Pastoral Care

Pastoral Care Revisited

Frank Wright

SCM PRESS LTD

Copyright © Frank Wright 1996

0 334 01199 X

First published 1996
by SCM Press Ltd
9–17 St Albans Place, London N1 0NX

Typeset at The Spartan Press Ltd,
Lymington, Hants
and printed in Great Britain by
Biddles Ltd, Guildford and King's Lynn

Contents

Introduction

This book is a revision, in one volume, of the three previous books I have written on pastoral care, together with some new material. It is based on the conviction that pastoral care is inescapably rooted in our human dependence on one another, and since it stems directly from the heart of Christian faith itself, must be a priority for every Christian and the church. It is intended for those who, lay and ordained, share that conviction.

The phrase 'pastoral care', however, causes me not a little hesitation. It can be construed as self-conscious and patronizing; it is now used in so many different contexts (for example: business, career guidance, and pupil management) that its essence can be much diluted; it might also suggest an irrelevant cosiness in the face of the enormity of social and personal ills which we face today. But despite those hesitations, I can find no better phrase than pastoral care to describe that which I see as central to faith and life.

This is no academic treatise, concerned with endless analyses or attempts to score debating points over other writers. Neither is it, on the other hand, a 'how to do it' manual, which would fail to do justice to the rich variety of person we meet in the different circumstances in which they are placed, and could not possibly catch the sensitivity which pastoral care always demands. Even if I had all the expertise necessary to deal with every kind of personal and social ill that afflicts us, this book is not that sort of comprehensive manual. There are specific areas which I have had to leave for those with specialized knowledge and experience. It is, I trust, well aware of our contemporary malaises and informed by some of the insights which recent theological thinking and the human sciences have given us – but beyond that, it is simply my reflections on my own pastoral experience in certain well-known areas, and on the wisdom provided for me by generations of students in university extra-mural courses I have taught, and by those with whom I have been involved in pastoral care and counselling.

My hope is that this book will give some slight encouragement, widen horizons and stimulate perseverance in those who believe, like me, that we all need to care more effectively with our heads as well as our hearts.

Fixed and Changing Contexts of Pastoral Care

A bishop, who is a long-standing friend of mine, used to join me in a walk in the countryside once a year. On one occasion, he had heard me preaching in the cathedral on the previous Sunday. 'Hearing you preach', he said, 'made me realize that you are a slimline Christian.' I don't think that he meant it as such, but I told him I thought it was a great compliment. For 'slimline' surely means having all superfluous fat cut away, being fitter, more adaptable, more ready to face the work that has to be done. And in a Christian sense, it surely means being willing to let go any excess Christian baggage and fruitless controversies, let go that which isn't essential to faith, and which is barely more than church paraphernalia. As the Bishop of Ely recently put it, 'We need have no hesitation in asserting that some matters in Christian faith and practice are more important than others.'[1]

That, then, is my stance: that of a slimline Christian, who is devoted to the core and centre of that faith, as he sees it. What is that core and centre? Christians may differ about the interpretation of what lies at the circumference, but what lies at the centre is surely indisputable, no matter what our ecclesiastical colours. 'At the heart of the universe, there is God, Unconditional Love, and this love we see supremely in the life, death and risen presence of Jesus Christ.' So, as John put it, 'We love because He first loved us.'[2] That unconditional love underpins the doctrine of grace, a word from the same root as gracious and graciousness, both sorely-neglected virtues today. And grace is to receive a kindness or goodness that we have done nothing to earn or deserve. As St Paul put it, 'While we were yet sinners, Christ died for us.'[3] Christians respond in gratitude to the grace which they have received through God's unconditional love in Christ, and which has so taken hold of them that they reflect to others something of that same unconditional love. So they are moved to a continuing attitude of care for others, and it becomes as natural for them to care as it is to breathe. And the paradox is that those who give pastoral care often feel that they receive greater love in return than that which they have initiated.

Not surprisingly, then, I warm to Alastair Campbell's definition of pastoral care: 'Pastoral care is, in essence, surprisingly simple. It has one fundamental aim: to help people to know love, both as something to be received and as something to give.'[4] Apart from its directness, this definition has another advantage: it doesn't shut off pastoral care as the special preserve of a few, and without any relationship to what else is going on both in society and in the church. It doesn't distinguish too sharply between those whose motivation is exclusively Christian, and those who don't in any sense share a Christian commitment. We need to affirm the value of every caring act, no matter what the motivation of the carer is – and in any case, how can any of us in post-Freudian times claim that our motives are pure and unmixed? Unselfconscious acts of pastoral care have their roots deep in the recognition of human interdependence, in humankind's instinct for community or simple humanity. In a Lancashire town a regular round of refuse collectors exchanged cheery words every week with the old ladies who inhabited a block of flats. When the round was changed, the ladies felt bereft. 'No one cares about us now,' they said.

Too much self-conscious theorizing about pastoral care can seem to undervalue the considerable amount of spontaneous caring that goes on unnoticed and unsung. Continuing support given to a colleague in the office when he or she is going through a divorce; a readiness to listen to the story of an acquaintance's depression: the list is endless. Horrifying stories of people passing by on the other side, in the face of some act of violence or personal tragedy, will receive a lot of media attention, but must always be balanced by those innumerable examples of corporate and individual care which receive no media attention at all. In the same town recently, where it was reported that two elderly widows had been mugged and assaulted, the first meeting of an informal befriending group was being held to arrange visits for the housebound of the neighbourhood. The first incident made headlines in the local newspaper, the second made no headlines at all.

Nor can we claim any superiority in caring done by Christians. The Christian temptation always to claim something 'a little bit extra that the others haven't got', as the old petrol advertisement had it, must always be resisted as an insult to the Holy Spirit who works in the world as well as in the church and whose influence can never be confined to those who wear the right label. All we can claim is that there is for the Christian a transcendent reality, which may be lacking in a secular situation of pastoral care, and a conviction that the path to wholeness is not purely of human endeavour and through the interaction of human beings. But it is sufficient that that dimension is silently present without any selfconscious references. God is still present, even when his name is not mentioned, and similarly, the encounter is not necessarily more religious when his name is constantly invoked.

That little word 'unconditional' in unconditional love is highly significant. It goes against the grain of much that is almost taken for granted in certain church circles. Consider: how would you react if you felt someone was being kind to you out of a sense of duty, to gain Brownie points, or worse still, to use that kindness as a bait to lure you into membership of an organization called the church? Instinctively, and quite rightly, you would rebel against such an insult to your personhood. You are being used as means to an end, which is an abhorrence to all Christian faith. I have known churches, conscious of declining membership, to fix on pastoral care almost as a gimmick to arrest that decline. That proves thoroughly counter-productive, and deserves to be.

Love, to be unconditional, must be freely given, freely received. And the love which issues in pastoral care is probably the most effective long-term evangelistic weapon which the church possesses – and it seems to have gone completely unnoticed in a Decade of Evangelism. Perhaps it isn't seen as such, because it is so long-term and is as far from conventional methods of evangelism as it could be.

But at a time when there is great suspicion of all oratory – not least, pulpit oratory – and cynicism about all institutions, and when the excitement of modern and technological advances and the dominance of material considerations often mask questions of meaning, purpose and value, only the demonstration of the quality of love inherent in pastoral care is likely to bite into contemporary hearts and minds. When a former Regius Professor of Modern History at Cambridge surveyed the action and interaction of Christian faith on the history of the world, he concluded that nothing but the spectacle of so much love coming into the world only to be crucified could move the stoniest of hearts. That still happens today when that love is incarnated in the nitty-gritty of pastoral care.

In the parish I served, we had a group of about twenty-four people who volunteered to be ready to help in any emergency. They didn't advertise or call themselves Good Samaritans or anything like that. But if I or a member of the congregation discovered anyone in need there they were – available. And it was one person's job, at the end of a phone, to match the person with the need. The Social Services Department in the Town Hall found it useful, too, to have resources they could call on when the need didn't fall within any well-defined category. I recall the time when one lady in her fifties in the parish – we'll call her Mrs Smith – fell victim to cancer, but was unwilling to go to hospital. Her husband's work took him away from home on occasions, and in order to provide day-to-day care, this group of volunteers took it upon themselves to organize a rota of helpers. Whenever I went to visit the patient, I never knew which member of the parish was going to open the door to me. They kept their rota going for something like six weeks till Mrs Smith died. And then quietly they withdrew. Now Mrs Smith wasn't a good churchgoer. She was the daughter of a churchwarden who was very good at pestering his friends and acquaintances to give money to the church, and both she and her husband had seen the church as a grabbing organization, a rather hard-faced institution. I'll never forget Mr Smith at the graveside. As soon as the service was over, he said to me how grateful he was to the people who had looked after his wife, and added, 'I never knew the church could be like that.' He'd undergone a revolution in the way he thought about it – not grabbing, but self-giving. No amount of talking would have convinced him, but caring in that sort of situation had made him think again. The caring wasn't done to impress him or convert him, simply for its own sake, and the result wasn't that Mr Smith came rushing to church every Sunday. As a matter of fact, he himself died two years later. But he had come to see that the church exists, like her Lord, for the sake of those who are in need. He came to glimpse something of the love which lies eternally in the heart of God.

That, then, is the enduring feature of pastoral care. What is its shifting context? The church and the world in which pastoral care operates today are light-years away, for instance, from George Herbert's and Richard Baxter's church and world of the seventeenth century, both of whom wrote treatises on pastoral care. Herbert in his *The Priest to the Temple* and Baxter in his *The Reformed Pastor* both saw the priest or minister as the only pastor – and omnicompetent at that, able to solve and resolve any or all of the human problems and dilemmas to which members of their congregations would be subject. Doctor, counsellor, solicitor, teacher, clergyman and friend – all to be found in one person. And one of the best-known clerics in the first half of this century, Canon Peter Green, Rector of St Philip's, Salford, was nearer in his approach to pastoral care to Herbert and Baxter in the seventeenth century than we are to him now in the church and world in which pastoral care has to operate. Wise and devoted though he was, there is no breath of suggestion in his writings on pastoral theology either that the laity should, at the very least, be partners in pastoral care, or that we might care more effectively if we paid heed to other insights derived from secular fields, rather than simple theological deductions.

Let us look a little more closely at these changes. An image with which I was encouraged in training for the ministry nearly fifty years ago was the Good Shepherd image from John 10, the obvious connection being that I, the ordained, was to be the pastor and the laity the sheep. Of course, that image still has much of value to say both to the ordained and the lay person. Our readiness in our pastoral work to be known as a person without any facade ('they know my voice'); our readiness to be available, and fully committed ('I lay down my life for the sheep'). But a simple comparison of ordained pastor and lay person with shepherd and sheep barely conceals notions completely unworthy of lay people, and sorely tempting to the ingrained authoritarian temper of clergy and ministers. And most clergy and ministers would surely readily admit that just as they minister to lay people, so they are ministered to by those same lay people. After eleven years, I was reluctantly moved out of the parish I was serving by a persistent bishop, in order to become a Residentiary Canon at the Cathedral. My pride made me wonder how the parish would survive without me, but I soon realized that the bereavement process was only mine and not theirs. I hadn't begun to realize just how well supported I'd been. I had just taken it for granted.

It has become a cliché to say that the role of clergy and ministers is to enable lay people in their work and witness: my impression and experience is that it can just as commonly happen the other way round. The future of pastoral care lies largely in the hands of the laity and from what I have seen, we haven't yet begun to tap their full potential in this respect. Take the question of bereavement: when I was ordained, I struggled with less and less success to keep in touch with those families with whom I had been involved in funerals. Today, it is often the laity who have taken on that responsibility. Some of the most encouraging meetings I have attended over the past five years have been the inaugural meetings of lay bereavement befrienders (I deliberately avoid the word counsellor) who, after a six-meeting course on the stages of bereavement and appropriate support, come alongside those who are grieving until, perhaps a year or eighteen months later, they reach the point of acceptance. Often hospices use lay people, after a period of training, to help those whose relatives have died there. Another example is of those teams of seven to ten parishioners in the Roman Catholic Diocese of Plymouth, who befriend one person with HIV and AIDS, working singly or in small groups, and who take it in turn to visit the sick person, do the household chores, or help with transport – and all this after attending one training day, and continuing in in-service training whilst they are working in their teams. These two examples could obviously be multiplied, illustrating the possibilities for rich pastoral care that exist, where there is vision and perseverance.

I mentioned earlier the writings of Canon Peter Green on church theology. There was never any suggestion in his writings of the way in which insights from secular fields could illuminate our pastoral caring. Of course, to be fair, the human sciences hadn't developed then to anything like their present extent. I often muse on the mistakes I might have avoided in my first halting steps in pastoral care, if I had had the advantage of reading some of the works that have been written since then (e.g. the classic works on bereavement of John Bowlby and Murray Parkes, Dorothy Rowe's book on depression, or Jack Dominian's work on marriage). To care is to love with the mind as well as the heart, to be ready to exercise all our faculties for the sake of others, to think hard about their needs and imaginatively to see things as they see them. And that, in turn, means being ready to learn about human beings and their needs from sources other than Christian faith itself. Indeed, pastoral theology, which systematizes pastoral care, is a putting together of these secular insights with the Christian doctrine of man, to arrive at a truth which will be fuller, richer and more whole than either would be left in isolation. It is a 'personalizing' of theology.

There have been recently, and still are, two other major shifts in the context of pastoral care and it may seem odd at first that I bracket them together. I refer to the declining membership of all the churches (except the Evangelical, Pentecostal and Charismatic churches) in the past twenty years, and the increasing need for pastoral carers to be political (small 'p'). Declining membership can have a disastrous effect on the church in three ways: first, it can become so concerned for its own institutional survival, and so turned inwards, that it loses all sense of mission, and by mission I don't simply mean evangelism, but the church's whole *raison d'etre*, to be the agent and servant of the Kingdom of God. Secondly, it can tempt the church to panic measures in order to ensure its survival, and use other ploys to attract members not so much for their own sake but simply as props towards that survival. Thirdly, it can exhaust the energies of a shrinking group of people in working to keep the doors open and the building heated so that there is no enthusiasm or energy left for looking outwards and serving the community in which the church is set. And that same shrinking group of people is often the same group most active individually in other community activities, like meals-on-wheels, work in the Citizens Advice Bureau and so on. So the church stands in judgment corporately on what Christ condemned individually: 'He who would save his life will lose it.'[5] I have nothing but compassion for those beleagured church members, pouring themselves out for something they truly believe in. But can institutional survival by itself ever be a legitimate Christian goal? Should it be our main anxiety? To go back to where we were earlier, isn't it our job simply to go on demonstrating the love of God without worrying about its outcome, firm in the faith that, in the end, we are utilizing the strongest force in the world? Dietrich Bonhoeffer was always keen to condemn what he called 'a church concerned primarily for its own self-preservation rather than its self-giving'. And that, as Bishop Butler said of enthusiasm, is 'a very, very horrid thing'. Bonhoeffer claimed in another place that 'the church is only the church when it exists for the sake of others', and in an oft-used quotation, Archbishop William Temple contended that 'the church is the one body which exists for the sake of those who do not yet belong'. There's a higher authority still: 'He who loses his life for my sake and the gospel will find it.'[6]

I want to return to the practical consequences for practical care this entails a little later, but now to that other item of the changing context of pastoral care: the need to become political. There has been a strong reaction, and rightly so in my view, against the excessively individualistic emphasis in pastoral care over the past thirty years, identified with the personal growth movement and what is popularly known as 'the me culture'. Most pastoral theologians agree that pastoral care has focussed too exclusively on ambulance work with people who are ill or in trouble whilst ignoring social, political and economic causes which are so often responsible for those ills and troubles. Indeed, it is possible to misuse pastoral care and counselling in order to avoid tackling fundamental political and social issues. It can become another up-dated version of Marx's 'opium of the people' if it ignores this political and social dimension. Indeed, Stephen Pattison has argued in a recent book[7] that the character and methods of liberation theology should be imported so that they might transform the theory and practice of pastoral care in the West and restore a proper social perspective.

Put baldly, what this means is that it is surely a luxury in a world where for every hour we spend agonizing over the details of someone's trouble at least another hundred children in the world, (and probably many more), will die of starvation. I am not for a moment trying to deny or under-estimate the distress or suffering through which people go: I am only suggesting that we restore the balance and give attention to helping cure some basic problem of need or social injustice, wherever it might be, rather than always being turned inwards towards some sophisticated personal dilemma. So there is always a broadly political (small 'p') dimension in pastoral care but it is always both/and with the person-to-person work and never either/or. That broadly political dimension enters into the way in which the church as a caring society sees its role in the community and not just with individuals.

So let us return for a moment to where we left off in our consideration of the church. Whenever I think of the church's social commitment to pastoral care, I have two images in front of me. The first goes back nearly fifty years to when I sat on the floor in the vicarage of down-town Darnall, near Sheffield, in the company of other theological students and some of the parishioners. They had been to Parish Communion on Sunday, and were now in the weekly Parish Meeting, the only church meeting in the week, since they were convinced that they should spend their time and make their witness in the world, at Trades Union meetings and the like, rather than talking about their own in-concerns of the church and church buildings. So they disposed of church business at the meeting as quickly as possible, studied the Bible for half an hour, and then turned to the local paper. Their question was, 'What should the church be doing about this, or this, or this?', and then they formulated a plan of action amongst themselves. The second image I have is of twenty years later when I was spending some time at Union Theological Seminary in New York. The well-known radical theologian of that time, Harvey Cox, took college prayers one morning. He brought in with him to chapel not a Bible or a Prayer Book but that morning's edition of the *New York Times*. He chose four items of news, and invited us to consider each item in the light of our Christian commitment. He gave us three minutes to do so after each item, followed by another five minutes silence, and then he departed. Put together Harvey Cox's emphasis on world issues and Darnall's insistence on local issues, and we get the balance roughly right.

So why doesn't each local church, or better still churches, in an area ask themselves three questions directly relevant to this social concern of pastoral care? First, what are the particular needs of this community which are not being met by any other social agency? Second, mindful of the warning given by Jesus about the man who started to build a tower, and couldn't complete it, what resources do we possess together to respond at least to some of those needs? Third, putting together both needs and resources, what strategy should we adopt so that we can respond to those needs to the best of our abilities? Elsewhere, of course, Christians with different ethical perspectives will also rightly be found in protest against what they perceive to be national and international evils, but those protests must always go hand-in-hand with rolling up our sleeves and tackling issues in our local community. Pastoral care, then, must always be balanced between care for the individual and social action.

Every age, as Adam said to Eve, is an age of transition, and we always have to beware doom-laden predictions about the future, as if the past had never happened. Bishop Lightfoot used to say of church history that it is a 'cordial for drooping spirits'. If that is true of church history it is even more true that a general historical perspective restores sanity and balance when the future of the world looks bleak. Nevertheless, it has to be conceded that we are living in an increasingly violent age, and that cynicism, general despair about the future and hopelessness are rife. Parents and grandparents frequently express fears for the welfare of their children and grandchildren in the twenty-first century. It was recently reported that a Brighton Council survey of teenagers of sixteen and nineteen years of age found that 'only one respondent out of 385 said that politics were important to them'. Such is the scale of apathy we encounter – and in my view, it surely has a lot to do with the impersonality, the devaluing of what it means to be a person, to be properly respected, and in the Christian tradition, to be reverenced as bearing God's image and loved by Him. No one can pretend that pastoral care can cure every human ill, or even in some cases, make any contribution at all to its resolution. What we are doing in pastoral care in a world of dehumanizing tendencies is asserting the unique value of the person.

To conclude, we have seen so far that pastoral care is to help people 'to know love as something to be received and something to give'; that the enduring feature of pastoral care for Christians is the motivation to reflect God's unconditional love to others, and that it becomes as natural for the Christian to care as it is for him to breathe; that pastoral care is the most effective evangelistic tool we possess, even though not executed for that purpose but simply for its own sake; that pastoral care today and in the future is, and will be, increasingly in the hands of the laity; that we need to be ready to learn from secular insights, as well as Christian theology, about the welfare of the person; that the declining membership of the church, and the need to be broadly political in pastoral care, should make us ask questions about how the church should best serve the community; and finally, that our work as carers isn't to heal every human ill but to keep alive in our world the dignity and value of the person.

2

Human Needs and our Response

Before we look further at what pastoral care is, we need to look at ourselves and our needs. If we are going to experience ourselves as full human beings, what needs must be satisfied? In so far as exercising pastoral care is using our imagination to try to respond to others' needs (and incidentally, perhaps, our own) we need to take account of the full range of those needs. Much misery and frustration, and worse, many neuroses, arise because we often limit need to the more obvious and easily visible: to take a commonplace example, what else ought we to worry about if we have food in our stomachs and a roof over our heads?

A model which has stood the test of time, and helps us to consider those needs, was given to us in the middle of this century by the psychologist Abraham Maslow, in what has become known as the 'hierarchy of human needs'.[1] The satisfaction of one need leads to the emergence of the next. First, there are our *physiological* needs, our need to be fed. Then there are our safety or *security* needs: the need to be able to live and work against a background of stability and an ordered world. As we travel further up the scale, our needs become more internal, relating more and more to our affections and emotions. So the next need is the need to *belong*. We all need to be able to feel at home in the company of a group (however small) of friends. If this need is supplied, then there emerge what Maslow calls our *esteem* needs, the need for a proper self-respect and for the respect of other people. And finally, there comes the need for what he calls *self-actualization*, 'to become everything that one is capable of becoming'. So Maslow's view is that there are these five levels of need: physiological, security, belonging, esteem and self-actualization. We need to look more closely at each level, to see how imaginative pastoral caring takes account of these needs, and could attempt to make a creative contribution in responding to them.

Perhaps we're less likely to fail to respond to obvious physiological needs than any other. Satiated as we may be by television coverage of famine-stricken areas and appeals from relief organizations, we can't help being moved by those who are suffering from extreme hunger. In this case, it's easy to take Maslow's point about the appearance of more needs only when other needs have first been satisfied. Paul VI in a papal encyclical said that a man 'must *know* something and *have* something in order to *be* something'. There is, in other words, a minimal subsistence line below which a person must not be allowed to go if he or she is to retain the dignity of being human. We sometimes put 'having' and 'being' in opposition to each other, but sometimes they are complementary. Ascetics can point to the spiritual benefits of fasting; hunger-strikers may be sustained by their passionate convictions; but to be consistently hungry often means a preoccupation with food which excludes all other preoccupations. The desire to eat becomes obsessive. I recall seeing Russian prisoners-of-war in Germany, not having the same Red Cross parcels as we occasionally did, prepared to tear each other limb from limb to win the prize of a few potato peelings rescued from our dustbins. William Golding's novel, *Lord of the Flies*, illustrates how, once both the constraints of civilization and food resources are removed, decent respectable people can come close to cannibalism. Hunger, voluntarily undertaken, may be spiritually beneficial; hunger imposed either by an enemy or by circumstances can degrade and dehumanize. Jesus in the Gospels seems to have had experience in himself and others of both sorts of hunger. He fasted and assumed that his disciples would fast: '*When* ye fast,' he said. But his injunction to give Jairus' daughter something to eat, and the feeding of the five thousand indicate how well he understood mankind's need for bread.

We may tire perhaps of the familiar and crude statistic, that two-thirds of the world's population goes to bed hungry, but – like the plight of the homeless begging in our cities – it should always prick our caring conscience. What is known as the 'poverty trap' catches more people in this country than is sometimes admitted. So pastoral

carers are bound to be ready to take initiatives in world development, and use political influence to ensure a more equitable
sharing of the world's resources.

When bodily needs are satisfied, security needs become
dominant. Recent surveys all indicate that violence heads the list of
people's anxieties. Again, as with hunger, unless our safety needs
are met to some degree, then the desire to meet those needs
becomes obsessive. A pensioner in Liverpool, whose flat on the
twenty-third storey of a council block has been twice vandalized
and herself beaten up, is unlikely to be ready to open the door to
anyone or move beyond the threshold. She will be a prisoner,
obsessed by her own fears and by the threats that anything outside
herself poses to her. Of course, feeling insecure takes many forms
apart from that of physical safety. My job may be insecure, I may
feel I am barely going to be able to provide for my family, my frail
health may let me down. It seems as if many fears we knew in
childhood carry over into our adult lives, and that even though we
may be better at handling them, they still never really disappear.
And there hangs over us all the black cloud of ecological disaster,
threatening to mock all our other safety needs. There is clearly an
uneasy balance between the safeguarding of our minimal safety
needs and living with essential insecurities. What does it mean
when we say that the final security of Christians is God, and
therefore they should be ready to take risks?

Prudent though we must be, we cannot, in the end, make
ourselves safe from all the possibilities of harm in the world.
Christian faith looks on the blackest of possibilities and still has to
say that nothing will finally separate us from God's love. We need,
as pastoral carers, to convey that ultimate assurance; but, for that
same reason, we must not become over-preoccupied with our
lesser safety needs. The gospel is about the business of going out
not knowing where we're going, of casting our bread on the waters,
of not burying our talent lest we lose it. Taking risks is at the heart
of the gospel, because God and his love can never be extinguished.
As Julian of Norwich pointed out a long time ago, we are not
promised immunity from the world's ills: we are promised that we
shall not be overcome – and that, because God is who he is.

In a relatively affluent society, it is perhaps the unfulfilment of our *belonging* needs, the unhappiness of our personal relationships, which causes more frustration than any other. But the word to 'belong' needs looking at. 'I need you in order to be myself' is an appropriate piece of shorthand for saying that properly to find ourselves, we need to lose our tightly-knit individual lives in the company of others and in the 'close' company of a few. Sometimes we confuse belonging and joining. Christians often feel that they must be in the joining business: that, rather like a jolly aunt at a children's party, the church must get everybody involved, and play the game together. But it's the sensitive child who rebels, and matiness isn't the goal of all our striving. Have we not sometimes frozen out of church life those who didn't express themselves in this way? The Parish Communion Movement, valuable though it has been, has sometimes given the impression that first-class Christians are to be found at *that* service, and those who prefer the quieter, older, more contemplative service are second-class.

My experience tells me that the world is full of people desperate not to join, but to belong. Their desperation drives them often to absurd devices, and sometimes humiliating, extreme gestures, in order to make that possible. There is a whole host of social factors making for this desperation: the break-up of traditional communities, the tendency for every industrial business undertaking to become larger and therefore more impersonal, the mobility of modern life, the generation gap. There is a great hunger for contact, belongingness, a need to overcome feelings of alienation and strangeness – especially as the world itself is getting a colder, uglier and more threatening place. Correspondingly, there is a great opportunity for the church to provide for the right sort of belongingness. It hasn't anything to do with getting people to join organizations; it has more to do with inviting people to come and feel warmly accepted in a small group of people who want to share their experiences of life, however different, and who are helped to believe that they have a contribution to make as well as a gift of friendship to receive. What the group *does* together is less important than what it *is*. If we're church members, we need to ask ourselves a penetrating question: supposing we didn't belong, but felt isolated and lonely, would the church attract us by its quality? Would we feel that we had come home, that this is where we truly belonged?

So we come to the most sensitive and painful area of all: the feeling that we have about ourselves and our worth as human beings. These are what Maslow calls our *esteem* needs, our desire for self-respect, self-esteem and the esteem of others, the necessity to feel that we count. This was well illustrated for me by a lady who was being visited in hospital by another member of the church congregation. 'Shall I tell the vicar you're in hospital?' she asked. 'Yes,' said the patient – and then quickly changed her mind. 'No,' she said, 'Let's see if he misses me . . . ' Experience has taught me that if all the people who are troubled or in despair could be assured that they have value as human beings, whatever their guilts, fears, unloveliness and feelings of uselessness, then they would be some way along the road to recovery. The trouble is that they often measure their own feelings of misery against the image of the successful portrayed in the media, the ideals held up to them by parents or conventional church teaching, or sometimes against the outward appearance of their acquaintances – and sink into further gloom. I have known several first-year university undergraduates who mistakenly think that all the others are coping well academically and living flourishing social lives, when really most of them are feeling isolated and alienated. Comparisons are always odious, but never more so than when we compare what we are and aren't with other people. Then we're denying that uniqueness which is ours through God's gift. Not to like oneself, not to love oneself, not to accept oneself, degenerates into hating oneself; and that is to enter into a pathological condition, whence all sorts of other ills flow. It is to arrive at the opposite of the truth on which Christian faith insists: that we are loved creatures of God, whoever or whatever we are. The truth, unfortunately, doesn't remain uppermost in people's perceptions. Often stretching back into childhood, there remains the image of an angry God who spies on you and decrees that some sins can never be forgiven. (I have known of one or two people who have mutilated themselves, or committed suicide, because they thought that they were guilty of the 'unforgivable' sin against the Holy Spirit.) God then becomes for the adult the God who rejects you rather than the God who accepts you, and other people's attitude towards you often seems to reinforce that conclusion. We all have things about us and in us which are unlovable; but the essential truth is that we are loved not for what we are or aren't, but just because we're there, made in God's image.

Sometimes going to church seems to make such people's difficulties hard to bear: the image of niceness, pleasantness, don't-we-have-fun-in-Christ's-family can make the person feel more isolated and different still. Exhortations they may hear there to be more loving, more faithful, increase their guilt or widen the gap between where they are and where they think other people are. Only genuine and patient pastoral care can bridge that gap. The truth that we are loved 'where we are right now', what I've called the essential Christian truth, has to be incarnated in the flesh and blood and spirit of one person or a small group of people who are prepared to take the time and trouble to understand what the other person is going through. Simply to listen fully and properly to another person's story sounds easy, but really to listen is a rare achievement, and it conveys to that person something of great value. Exercises have sometimes been used, in the practice of group dynamics, in which time has been spent by members of the group just looking at each other, finding something 'nice' to say about each other, genuinely appreciating each other – on the assumption that 'there's a beautiful person struggling to get out'. (God's image?) If we could translate that self-conscious exercise into our everyday dealings with other people, we should begin, quite unselfconsciously, to heal some of their wounds.

This knowledge of our self worth assumes greater significance still because of the world in which we live. It has been generally true, since the Industrial Revolution, that society has increasingly seen men and women as functionaries, economic units, there to keep 'the wheels of industry turning'. So a person becomes important, not intrinsically, not in themselves, but in so far as they make a practical contribution to a world of production. That is a deeply ingrained assumption, which has religious roots in a Calvinistic ethic of the importance of work, and which found some earlier justification in Paul's 'if a man doesn't work, neither shall he eat.'[2] The modern version is the vilification of shirkers and scroungers. (This is not to deny that there are some, but simply to point to the way in which we use the economic yardstick to estimate worth.) Perhaps we can see how false and damaging this hidden assumption is when we consider those who are handicapped. Realistically speaking, a handicapped person may not make any practical contribution to the prosperity of the country; indeed he or she will probably have to take from the resources of the welfare state in order to survive; but it would be difficult to find anyone who didn't believe that handicapped people are valuable, just because they *are*. Numbers of parents of handicapped children testify that, despite all their disabilities, the children have given them much more than they, as parents, have given to the children.

Judging people's worth by their functioning is responsible for much hidden misery in the world. It often lies behind the trauma associated with unemployment, redundancy and retirement, and makes the pains of sick people hard to bear. And aren't the forecasts for the future – little chance of full employment for large sections of the population, no more job security for life, shorter working hours, greater leisure, and so on – all pointing to the necessity to expose this assumption? Christian truth about the worth of every individual, irrespective of their gifts or lack of them, their proper functioning or not, was never more topical or relevant than it is today. It wouldn't be too much to claim that in it lies the only hope for a healthy society of the future.

When those four basic needs – physiological, security, belonging and esteem – are satisfied, one may well wonder what others there could possibly be! Their satisfaction constitutes the acme of average expectations. Perhaps our temptation is to get stuck in the gratification of lower needs in the hierarchy, especially in days and areas of deprivation, in the same way in which it is the church's temptation to get stuck in the business of organization and administration. In both cases we are surrendering to a diminished view of life, and settling for what has so often been castigated by Christians (though the phrase needs qualification) as a 'materialistic way of life'. ('A pleasant semi-detached, in a nice area, money for holidays and Christmas, family catered for, a few good friends, and well thought of – what more is there to life? What else should I worry about?') The

mounting incidence of mental illness, the frustration and restless-
ness of so many people, point to the truth that we all have a need
within us to be what we must be. Maslow insists that what a person
can be, they must be. That is, must be true to their own nature.
Following another psychologist, Goldstein, he calls this process of
self-fulfilment 'self-actualization'; and he instances how in one
individual it may take the form of being a good mother, in another an
athlete, in another an artist, and so on. And when Maslow looked at
those deemed to be psychologically healthy, old and young, together
with certain characters from history, he discovered that these 'self-
actualizers' displayed certain characteristics in common. What those
characteristics are, and how close they come to the character of
Jesus, we shall explore in the next chapter. Sufficient here to notice
that 'psychologically healthy' doesn't mean 'well-adjusted' in the
sense the phrase is usually meant to convey: easy, amiable,
predictable, never standing out in any way. Those adjectives could
hardly be said to apply to the Jesus who didn't always make things
easy for others because he consistently spoke the truth, and whose
insights into other people's characters scarcely made him amiable on
occasions. His spontaneous reaction to others' needs as he saw them
robbed him of being predictable; he could be described as eccentric,
and his eccentricity led him to his cross. Such was his 'self-
actualization', and it was the opposite of the cool, 'well-adjusted'
person. There are other grounds for 'being awkward' than psychological disturbance: it may be rather a sign of health and wholeness.
Saints aren't always easy to live with.

This, I think, says a great deal about the way we are to care, and
what our caring should be helping other people to become:
genuinely themselves. We are not trying to make them pale
imitations of us. In all our caring, we are helping to set free someone,
something that is unique in the universe, a creation of God who is to
be fulfilled in that potential which God implanted, and which is a
person's special and eternal destiny.

There is, then, a response which our pastoral care can make at
every level of human need identified by the psychologists, a response
(I would claim) which is potentially made richer and more effective
through Christian motivation and insights. But it must be caring for

its own sake, and not with the conscious or unconscious aim of making those cared-for into Christians. Otherwise, we are subtly slipping over into treating people as means, even if the ends are worthy. The way in which we exercise such unconditional care speaks powerfully for the gospel, and it has often been tragically true that Christians have denied the content of the gospel they are proclaiming through the methods they employ to do so. Christians may rightly feel that every man and woman has a need for the gospel of Jesus Christ, and that this is surely an omission in Maslow's scheme. But, I would see that gospel operating at every level of human need, rather than at one stratum of it, or at a different level altogether.

Finally, lest it be thought that we have been taking Maslow's model too literally, it needs to be said that it is imprecise, and that no one would suggest, least of all Maslow himself, that his scheme is that into which we all fit, that we must *all* have *all* our lower needs satisfied before we proceed to the next stage. The truth is that we are partly satisfied in our basic needs, and partly unsatisfied at one and the same time. Nevertheless, it is still, I believe, very helpful as a dynamic, but inevitably rough, model of the needs pastoral care seeks to respond to, and as some means of checking our effectiveness.

In our consumer society, there is a deal of confusion between needs and wants. High-pressure advertising and salesmanship convince us that we badly need something which countless generations have managed very well without, and our wants become our needs. Our greed is disguised as our need. It is all the more necessary, therefore, to have as clear a view as possible of basic human needs, and the most effective way of responding to them.

3

Caring and Growth

At the beginning of this century the Professor of Moral and Pastoral Theology in the University of Oxford gave this advice to his students: 'Do not visit parishioners on Mondays – it's Washing Day. They will not wish to see you, and the steam can be very unpleasant.'[1] Now that practical approach to practical matters, though softened a little by less class rigidity, was still characteristic of ordination training in my day: how to hold the baby when baptizing, how to conduct yourself when travelling back in the hearse after the funeral, how to avoid the perils of visiting an unmarried lady in her bedsit. But questions of meaning, purpose and value, basic questions like 'What's the point of it all?', seemed to be completely ignored. So in the early days of my ministry I began my search for an answer to that fundamental problem.

The first clue I discovered in an unlikely place: a Pastoral Letter of Cardinal Suhard, Archbishop of Paris, in the late 1940s. 'It is the pastoral task and privilege', he said, 'to keep the mystery of God present to man.' And he added, even more challengingly, that means 'so to live one's life that it would be inexplicable if God did not exist'. (Incidentally, I always think there is enough force in those words to make one reflect for many months on one's own personal qualities.) So I began to see that if the pastoral carer is unselfconsciously pointing towards the mystery of God through his or her stance in pastoral matters and the quality of his or her own life, then they will also see themselves as enablers of vision for other people, and hence, enablers of personal growth. Pastoral care, wrote R. A. Lambourne, who was both a medical doctor and a theologian, is 'a pattern of corporate, responsible, sensitive acts motivated by a compelling vision'.[2] That 'compelling vision' is crucial, as we shall see later.

What was puzzling to me was the way in which I only heard later, or rather read of the term 'personal growth' not in the church at all, but in the writings of the humanistic psychologists like the Americans Abraham Maslow, whose 'hierarchy of human needs' we explored in the last chapter, Carl Rogers or Gordon Allport, and our own English Anthony Storr. I began to sense that this was just one more example of a secular movement catching the church bathing and running away with our clothes. For the necessity for personal growth, the journey or pilgrimage to sanctification, is undoubtedly there in our Christian title deeds. St Paul writes in the first letter to the Corinthians of 'having to grow up from being a child, and having to put away the child's outlook and thoughts'.[3] And in his letter to the Ephesians he speaks of our vocation to grow 'to mature manhood, measured by nothing less than the full stature of Christ'.[4] And what does this growth to mature manhood entail? Being 'shaped to the likeness of God's Son', he tells the Romans.[5]

Now I want to explore the implications of this a little later. But notice, for the moment, how this emphasis on the necessity for growth has been overshadowed, if not almost obliterated, by concerns for the institutional church. When I look back to the early days of my ministry I realize how subtly and sometimes not so subtly I had been encouraged to think that my prime loyalty was to the welfare of the institution: that the church should grow numerically (if not also financially). Such concerns of the institution are still, as I have already indicated, over-dominant in the Christian scene. The impression often given to church members is that once you have made the difficult decision of faith, and come into the Body of Christ, nothing else remains to be done except perhaps to keep faithfully where you are, and above all not to go missing. The traditional Christian notion, embedded in the New Testament, and the most important strand in the early church, is its focus on our journey of love towards the vision of God. The idea that we are going somewhere as Christians, on a journey of growth and exploration, seems to have been lost. Moreover, my constant experience over these past years has been to hear good Christian people from different social backgrounds and churches telling me that they realize they are not being fed by their church membership and not being given space and opportunity to grow. There is, it seems to me, too much kindly but mistaken tolerance of spiritual mediocrity about today. It was the German philosopher Nietzsche who rejected Christian faith not so much on philosophical grounds, but because the Christians he met were so mediocre spiritually. I know it is a subjective and very possibly illegitimate judgment to make, but pastorally speaking, I have for a long time been troubled by a persistent question. How can it be that some communicants receive the sacrament every week for years without it seeming to make any apparent difference to the quality of their personal life: their lack of openness, their prejudices, their complacency? And allied to that, what does it say about the quality of the church's life when, as I observed in my own parish, so many parishioners came to church once and never came back again? Clearly, they were not held or gripped by the vitality of the worship or the richness of the individual and corporate lives they found there. Perhaps I labour the point too much, but it is something I feel very strongly about, this tolerance of spiritual mediocrity. Sometimes we develop a sorry complacency about being 'little people' and come to believe that it is the big people who do most harm in the world, and that if all the big people were only little people, then mankind would be happy. This is a parody of Christian humility. Our destiny is not littleness but greatness: predestined for glory, growing through the Christian life towards that maturity and sanctification, that transfiguration of human reality in the Kingdom of God, which is his purpose for us all.

Now my contention would be that just as it is easy for the church to settle for institutional concerns, so it is tempting for those of us who are involved in caring and counselling to be preoccupied with crises and problems. In other words, our temptation is to concentrate on segments of people's lives and experience without exploring any further the ultimate goal of all our pastoral care and counselling, and see it as the growth to wholeness and the maturity of the other person. In his classic work *The Integrity of the Personality*, Anthony Storr wrote that it is 'unscientific' to omit mention of goals in describing human behaviour, and Abraham Maslow calls the process of 'self-actualizing' or maturity the goal of human striving. I want to suggest that we can all too easily in our work simply respond to the needs of the moment. But in my experience, the longer term perspective of growth to maturity delivers the pastoral carer from the necessity to see immediate results that are too easy, too facile, and saves him or her from short-termism and sustains faith and hope in the enterprise.

What is this maturity towards which we journey, and how can it be characterized? I shall not easily forget the mounting excitement I felt on reading the humanistic psychologist's description of the maturing or self-actualizing person, to realize that there was a certain correspondence between the psychological goal of maturity and the Christian goal of sanctification. There is a common portrait which, however independently they work, humanistic psychologists and Christians paint of maturing people. They will be those who are prepared to accept themselves without feeling guilty or defensive; there is about them a naturalness, a simplicity, a spontaneity, an absence of artificiality and a refusal to be bound by convention. They usually have 'a mission in life', orientated to people and causes outside themselves, which will absorb much of their energy. They will actually like being on their own, but they will also be able to have especially deep relationships with just a few people. They will be independent of other people's good opinions, or even their attention, and they will not be slaves to their environment. They will have a sense of humour that will be 'philosophical and non-hostile'. They will relate to others irrespective of race, class, education or religion. They will have an appreciation of the ordinary things in life. When they see a new born baby for the thousandth time it will be just as wonderful as if they were seeing one for the first time. They will be able to lose themselves in some enjoyment of music or reading, some aesthetic, mystical or sexual experience. Now I wonder if you can in this description make connections with what you would conceive to be the way in which the Christian character shows itself in human life? Such a similarity between the portrait of psychological and Christian maturity I find fascinating, a strong witness to the fact that whatever language we use to describe it, and from whatever disciplinary perspective we come from, all truth is in the end One Truth.

Such maturity is not to be equated with moral perfection, even if such a state of mind ever existed or could exist. As Harry Williams said in his collection of sermons called *True Wilderness*, 'When we look at the New Testament, we find a Christ who did not always do the ideal thing. We discover that the notion that He did is wishful thinking – a refusal to accept the full fact of His humanity. For in human life it is generally not possible to do the ideal thing. The claims men have to meet very often clash with each other, so that you cannot give to every claim what is due.'[6] And Harry Williams went on to instance the way in which Jesus gave himself to his work at the expense of his family, and the way in which Jewish scholars have accused him of being so concerned to proclaim his own message that he was sometimes unfair to his opponents. So the mature person is not the ideal person, the one who from a particular moral standpoint has achieved perfection. In any case, Jesus' command 'Be Ye perfect',[7] the command which has caused such feelings of inadequacy and guilt in so many good people, should really be translated 'be rounded, complete, mature'. And maturity can never be seen as a fixed, predictable goal or static point. Rather it is a road, a direction of movement: hence Abraham Maslow's insistence on self-actualizing rather than self-actualization; hence the Christian insistence on the *road* to wholeness.

Here perhaps a word of caution is desirable about our use of the word 'saint' to describe the goal of human and Christian endeavours, since the word is patent of so much confusion and misunderstanding. For some time I had a cartoon on my office notice board which depicted a middle-aged married couple enjoying the sort of confrontation which is designed to release some of their frustrations with each other. The husband glares across at his wife and says 'When someone asks me what you're like, I tell them you're a saint – and that usually shuts them up!', and I notice that in her biography of her husband, pacifist and well-known CND activist Canon John Collins,[8] Diana, his widow, says of him that he was a very good man but not a saint. Chiefly, apparently, on the grounds that he liked good wine, cigars and gossip! But it does illustrate the way in which we are not talking of sinlessness when we are talking of saint, cardboard characters rather than real people. St Paul was touchy, vain and

quarrelsome; St Peter lacked moral fibre, as we used to say in the
Royal Air Force, not only when the cock crowed, but also after the
resurrection, when he refused to stand by his convictions about
Gentile Christians. It seems to me that the church has often
presented saints as people not conditioned by the same physical and
psychological forces which operate on the rest of us, whereas in
practice they are involved not just in temptation to sin, but also to
boredom and depression, just as we are. Perhaps we need to see
sainthood above all as 'ordinary, that is ordinariness so much loved
and treasured, so much polished and cherished, that it becomes
extra-ordinary'.[9] Obviously we need models of sanctity and maturity, but models are for inspiration, not for imitation. (We are not to
imitate Christ, but to be inspired and challenged by him.) And once
we see the character of Jesus as our inspiration, we shall not be
dictated to by literalism or constrained by legalistic detail. We will
not be over-anxious about the effects of Gospel criticism or our lack
of certainty of what we know about the earthly life of Jesus. We will
be spontaneous in following him and not succumb in any sense to
spiritual pride, or the feeling that we have arrived. If it be objected
that our portrait of Christ is subjective, we should accept the
criticism – but not wholly so. We do have some standard reference in
the Gospels.

Perhaps we can begin to see sainthood or sanctity as some aspect
of the character of Christ shining in and through a person. Then we
shall allow for the great diversity of all those who are called to be
saints. In other words not how alike saints are to each other, but how
unlike they are. The theologian Paul Tillich used to say that the
distinctiveness of the unity of the church lies in its power to take to
itself more diversity. And that means that we are, in our own work as
pastoral carers, to coax different seeds of growth in the people we
care for, until they reach a maturity, that richness of character, their
own particular character and no one else's.

How, then, are we to be in our caring work the agents of such
maturity and sanctity? We need, first, to do all we can to further adult
education. And by adult education, I do not mean handing down
dogmatic answers to dispose quickly of awkward questions. I am not
thinking either of detailed biblical knowledge so beloved of quizzes,

or the history of Christian doctrine or the liturgy of the fourth century. Very little is needed by way of such knowledge: the ability to use the Bible intelligently, see its different parts and its cultural relativism in perspective, and have sober expectations of it. It is rather the questions which come out of our daily experiences which provide the syllabus: that morally grey area, in which if we are honest we would admit that we are constantly immersed. (How often does it need to be recognized that the New Testament gives us direction, but not *directions* in these moral dilemmas?) If, for instance, relationships are to be fulfilling, and relationship has been a key word to several twentieth-century theologians, then what relationships and how far can they be taken? What too of my Christian social responsibility? My experience is that the considerable help which the adult Christian requires cannot, because of the inherent structures, come to him or her through the conventional teaching channels of the church. Exposure to worship, even if liturgically experimental, invariably reinforces Christian imperialist assumptions. The very solemnity with which the Word is read continually raises false expectations as to what Bible reading can accomplish; no preaching from the pulpit can deal adequately or sensibly enough with the moral dilemmas posed in the real lives of the congregation. The logic is inevitable. At a time when all secular non-vocational adult education is under threat financially, it is incumbent upon us to find the opportunities in our church weekends, or teaching weeks and house groups, to generate such a sense of freedom and openness that people of all sorts will be able to express their convictions and reflect on what matters to them both in Christian faith and in their own personal lives. I remember well how at one meeting of a Lenten course on 'Contemporary Belief', a churchwarden was moved to say that although he had been coming to church for years, he had never discovered 'who this God was' or where he could find him – and then, as if he had surprised himself by his willingness to be so honest and courageous, he added 'You know, that's the first time I've been able to say that.' At that point, although the course was half over, real communication could begin. That was the beginning of liberation for him, an initial step in his personal growth.

Now in saying all this I am suggesting that there is a real analogy between the role of the carer and that of the educator. We are both agents of change, facilitators of growth, stimulators of vision. My point is that because we as carers see how essential is a concern for personal growth, we will always be ready to further, wherever we can, initiatives in adult education.

There is no need, I am sure, to do any more than glance at my second point. I mean the subtle, insidious temptations to power inherent in all our caring, and especially in the attraction of allowing other people to be dependent upon us. I wonder about that attraction: is it the power it gives us or are we using the other person and the help and care we offer as a very attractive way of hiding from ourselves our own considerable and deep personal needs? One thing, I think, is obvious. We can, yielding to the subtle temptations to encourage dependency, preclude growth in the person we seek to help.

My third point is inter-connected with the last. That is, that in our dealings with other people, we should treat them as if they were mature. Now this is a difficult truth to demonstrate and substantiate – and I am not even sure that it can be – because it simply springs directly from experience. There are many temptations to short-circuit problems by suggesting, or even imposing, resolutions of our own, because in the end we think we know best. It isn't too difficult even to slip into a sort of feeling that we are indispensable to the other person. (I will always be grateful to the first organist with whom I served who once took me out to the graveyard and said to me rather gloomily, 'that place is full of indispensables'.) Confronted by what is obviously feckless ignorance or lack of intelligence, we can easily persuade ourselves that it would be folly to let decision-making go out of our hands. But in the end it is just another facet of our own inner urge to keep people dependent. As parents painfully come to see, growth happens when children are allowed to make mistakes, and are still supported through them. We have to learn to live with apparent impotence, but it is only apparent. Let me give you two examples: to someone eaten up by loneliness, in the end the most we can sometimes do is to help the person accept the loneliness, or at least their aloneness, as part of what it means to be a human being.

We cannot, like the medical profession, offer tranquillisers to ease the pain. And secondly, for example, there is no point and possibly evasion in simply listing compensations, for instance, that a bereaved person may have (other relatives, children, financial security, a cherished place in the community and so on) when the basic problem is coming to terms with the personal loss which the death has brought about. There is obviously a place for temporizing in our caring but if it continues indefinitely, it is treating adults as children and keeping them immature.

I suggest, then, that we have an eye to the potential for growth in adult education; are aware of our subtle temptation to power which will block the other person's growth; and thirdly, that we treat other people as if they were mature. My fourth point brings us right back to what and where we are as persons. Our caring concerns are as much to do with being as with doing. It is in small ways and little things that we hinder or help another person's development or growth. Just as children learn most from parents not so much from what they say or command but what they are in their unguarded moments and consequently try to imitate, so it is with us. Our spontaneous attitude, our unspoken values, our ways of approaching things, will be as influential for the other person's growth as any formal situation in which we are involved with them. Whether we like it or not, we inevitably become a model of some sort for the other person, however genuine, accepting and empathic we are. If we are seen as someone seeking to pursue the road to wholeness for ourselves, we will quite naturally be helping the growth of the other person.

There is, however, a final twist to the tale. I have spoken all the way through about a sort of correspondence between the goal of psychological maturity and that of Christian sanctification. But once we ask the question, 'How is personal growth achieved?', a divide sharply opens up. In Brian Thorne's recent biographical appraisal of the life and work of Carl Rogers, he refers to a book written some time ago by Paul C. Vitz, who is Associate Professor of Psychology at New York University. The book is called *Psychology as Religion: The Cult of Self-Worship*. Vitz puts his finger on the difference between the two approaches: within psychology, 'the relentless and single minded search for a glorification of the self is at direct cross purposes with the Christian injunction to lose the self'. And he goes on, 'What is excluded is a spiritual life of prayer, meditation and worship – the essential vertical dimension of Christianity, the relation to God.' 'Selfism is an example of a horizontal heresy, with its emphasis only on the present and on self-centred ethics. At its very best (which is not often) it is Christianity without the First Commandment.'[10] So Paul C. Vitz. The Christian on the other hand cannot relentlessly pursue his own growth. He or she should obviously be concerned but also paradoxically unconcerned. Concerned that his or her growth towards the embodiment of Christ's love and life takes place within him or her, unconcerned in that so long as he or she simply places the emphasis on growth, that growth is unlikely to happen. We must not be taking our spiritual temperature all the time, for that is to concentrate on the self and is death to growth. 'Is there a man among you', said Jesus, 'who by anxious thoughts can add a foot to his height?'[11] As Christians, we do not happen to be looking at ourselves; we are taken up by the vision of God's love in Christ, and the measure of our response to that vision of love will be the measure of our growth. It will be the journey to that vision which we still find ourselves taking, where our lives are hidden with Christ in God and in prayer, sacrament, meditation and silence. Unlike the psychological model, we will not be trying to make something of ourselves; rather, we will be giving ourselves space and discipline to be made by him.

The curse of the contemporary emphasis on personal growth is its narcissism; the secret of growth and sanctification is to abandon every effort to cultivate the self, or in a simpler formula still, coming right from the heart of the gospel, it is to lose oneself to find oneself.

4

Ambiguities in our Caring

What impels us to care? Are we clear about our motives? The careful screening that takes place in some voluntary organizations to ensure that the motivations of volunteers are sound is obviously essential: the potential for damage that rests within anyone who tries to manipulate people for his or her own ends is frightening in such a sensitive area as ours. I recall the immense harm done in another context by a well-intentioned married lady without children who, in consequence of her own maternal deprivation, smothered the boys in a Bible class – and she did not begin to recognize the truth of the situation.

But that isn't quite the whole story. The most rigid screening will never reveal the complexities of our hidden and mixed motivations, and living as we do in a post-Freudian age, none of us can truly doubt that mixed motivation. Let me give you an example from my own vocation. Traditionally, that vocation to the priesthood has been seen as a clear light, a divine call – comparable in its directness to Isaiah's vision in the temple: 'here am I; send me'. But several years ago a survey was done into the reason why some ministers chose their vocation. And the conclusions it reached were only at first surprising. It was, it concluded, because of a 'love-deprivatory' experience as children. All of us instinctively recognize the need to be loved and the only way in which we can ensure that love is first, to go out ourselves in love for others. So, if we have been inadequately loved as children, for some reason or another, we may try to over-compensate by our own loving in order to be loved. Now you can soon see that if you institutionalize that over-compensation, the caring organizations like the ministry have a great attraction. I have to say that if I dare to look at my own autobiography, that is largely true of me, and it may also be true of most of us in the caring professions, voluntary or otherwise. But once we recognize it and accept it, it need cause us no more anxiety. We are all in the same boat of mixed motivation, and if we look a bit further we will also see that it has the great merit of keeping us humble, not becoming the great and important Helper (big H) over and above the helped (small h). Have there not been times when the prospect of a difficult visit to befriend has daunted and depressed us? And yet afterwards we often feel better and more whole as a human being because we have received as well as given. There is a mutuality about all caring which again, once we acknowledge it, gives us a sense of modest proportion about ourselves. The hand I stretch out in caring is not completely unlike the hand of the one who will respond to it.

However, the hands which are stretched out vary enormously in contours, shapes and sizes – and rightly. We are all individuals with different backgrounds and temperaments, different characteristics and deficiencies, together (thank God) with different gifts. I plead no justification for the bumbling amateur when I say that in days of increasing professionalism, especially in the caring professions, we need to beware a sort of strait-jacket professionalism which in the end would reduce us all to puppets and iron out any eccentricity or quirk of individuality. Of course, we all need guidelines, but the befriending and pastoral role, wherever and whenever it operates, is an exercise involving two real people and the quality of the encounter between them. If the befriender or carer is not really seeing or hearing the other person but responding in the cliché-ridden manner which he or she deems to be appropriate to the guidelines they have been taught, then there will be little meeting and very little achieved. I alluded earlier to Carl Rogers, who stresses the importance of being a genuine person in the counselling role. I especially warmed to the way in which at one point he says that occasionally in an interview, he has been able to express his real feeling of boredom with the repetitious material with which the client is presenting him. I have never felt bold enough to say to anyone something like this: 'Come on, old chap, I'm bored with this, let's move it on a bit.' But I completely take his point about genuineness and naturalness. For a long time I had doubts about one particular volunteer bereavement counsellor in a team with which I was working. Kind and avuncular though he was he never seemed to be afraid of being both judgmental and directive, two characteristics I have always quite naturally disliked in any field of human relationships. But I was very much reminded of how generous we need to be in our discernment when, on three different occasions, I received the warmest letters of thanks from those whom Joe (we'll call him) had helped and I realized what patience and trouble he had taken in each case, at no small cost to himself. There are always, of course, dangers in allowing the free play of individuality, especially when working in an area as sensitive as ours, and the risks are too great to be ignored. But in the end, all that we have to offer, even in the most delicate of situations, is an outstretched hand, warts and all: our weaknesses, our hidden fears and anxieties, perhaps our lifelong sadnesses, as well as our strengths. And the paradox is that in our weakness lies our strength.

It is those who are willing to let go pretences who help most. Monica Furlong's poem, 'A Slum is Where Somebody Else Lives' makes this point:

A slum is where somebody else lives,
Help is what others need.
We all want to be the priest, social worker, nurse,
The nun in the white habit giving out the soup –
To work from a position of power,
The power being
That we are not the shuffler in the queue
Holding out his bowl.
But there is only one way into the kingdom
– To be found out in our poverty.
That is why the citizens are a job lot –
Unhappily married, the feckless mother of eight,
The harlot no longer young,
The lover of little girls, the sexually untameable,
The alcoholic, the violent, and those whose drink is
    despair.
Show me not, Lord, your rich men

With their proud boasts of poverty and celibacy
They are too much for me.
Hide me from those who want to help
And still have strength to do so.
Only those who get on with their lives
And think they have nothing to give
Are any use to me.
Let your bankrupts feed me.[1]

The paradox seems to be not only that there is no helping without being helped, but also that sometimes it is when we are feeling most unhelpful, even helpless, that we are of most help – providing we do not shrink from the feeling of helplessness, and attempt to minimize it by an attitude of defensiveness. The mode of Jesus' ministry, chosen in the wilderness, contained within it this potential of helplessness. In Gethsemene, that choice is reaffirmed, and then he experiences the physical helplessness of torture and crucifixion and the mental and spiritual helplessness of feeling abandoned by his father, expressed in his cry of dereliction. He dies, powerless, helpless – by choice. His death is the direct result of the decision he had taken in the wilderness and pursued throughout his ministry. Yet it was at this point of helplessness that God seemed to bring new meaning out of his life. The victory of the resurrecton is in part, a victory of the way of helplessness, a confirmation of the mode of Jesus' ministry. The glory of God is seen not in contrast to helplessness but through it. When I taught, on the clinical training course, nursing staff who were changing from hospital work to hospice work, one of their main anxieties was their feeling of total inadequacy in coping with the challenge. My response was always the same: 'God preserve us from all those who feel adequate!' In any case, who can properly feel adequate in facing the mystery of death? Once we assume our own adequacy, we are lengthening the gap between our strengths and the other person's feelings of weakness and pain and despair, and so reducing our capacity to show empathy; and we are trampling on the mystery of the person and human relationships, as if we had within us something of the divine omniscience.

There is a further danger: that of the so-called 'bedside manner', a benevolent and cheerful despotism, which tries to smooth over difficulties and cover over chasms of suffering, pain and anxiety with enforced heartiness. This 'bedside manner' suppresses individuality and attempts to bring about a uniformity of response in the patient so that the helper can feel 'safe'. It is another defence against feeling threatened and helpless. Sydney Jourard, in his book *The Transparent Self*, says that he knows of several instances of people who nearly died because 'every time they tried to tell their nurse of their intolerance of penicillin, the nurse replied, cheerfully and firmly, as she neatly performed the injection, "the doctor knows what's best; this will help to get you well". Nobody listened.'[2] Brian Clark's play, *Whose Life is it Anyway?*, makes the same point under a different guise. In the play the chief character, Ken, a sculptor, has been the victim of a severe road accident and is paralysed from the neck down. The hospital doctors take it for granted that once his condition is stabilized, he will be transferred to another unit and so, technically speaking, be kept alive. Ken, with ice cool clarity, argues from his bed that he should be allowed to die. Mrs Gillian Boyle visits Ken. She is a medical social worker and described as, 'thirty five, attractive and very professional in her manner'.

Mrs Boyle:	Good morning.
Ken:	Morning.
Mrs Boyle:	Mr Harrison?
Ken:	(cheerfully) It used to be.
Mrs Boyle:	My name is Mrs Boyle.
Ken:	And you've come to cheer me up.
Mrs Boyle:	I wouldn't put it like that.
Ken:	How would you put it?
Mrs Boyle:	I've come to see if I can help.
Ken:	Good. You can.
Mrs Boyle:	How?
Ken:	Go and convince Dr Frankenstein that he has successfully made his monster and he can now let it go.

Mrs Boyle:	Dr Emerson is a first-rate physician. My goodness, they have improved this room.
Ken:	Have they?
Mrs Boyle:	It used to be really dismal. All dark green and cream. It's surprising what pastel colours will do, isn't it? Really cheerful.
Ken:	Yes; perhaps they should try painting me. I'd hate to be the thing that ruins the decor.[3]

As the conversation proceeds and Ken's frustrations make him more bitter:

Ken:	It's marvellous you know.
Mrs Boyle:	What is?
Ken:	All you people have the same technique. When I say something really awkward you just pretend I haven't said anything at all. You're all the bloody same . . . Well there's another outburst. That should be your cue to comment on the lightshade or the colour of the walls.
Mrs Boyle:	I'm sorry if I have upset you.
Ken:	Of course you have upset me. You and the doctors with your appalling so-called professionalism, which is nothing more than a series of verbal tricks to prevent you relating to your patients as human beings.
Mrs Boyle:	You must understand; we have to remain relatively detached in order to help . . .
Ken:	That's alright with me. Detach yourself. Tear yourself off on the dotted line that divides the woman from the social worker and post yourself off to another patient.
Mrs Boyle:	You're very upset.
Ken:	Christ Almighty, you're doing it again. Listen to yourself woman. I say something offensive about you and you turn your professional

> cheek. If you were human, you'd tell me to
> bugger off. Can't you see that this is why I've
> decided that life isn't worth living? I am not
> human and I'm even more convinced of that
> by your visit than I was before, so how does
> that grab you? The very exercise of your so-
> called professionalism makes me want to
> die.[4]

Mrs Boyle clearly erred on the side of feeling 'relatively detached
in order to help'. A measure of detachment is clearly essential in our
caring, but somewhere the line has to be drawn between 'involvement' and 'detachment', and effective caring requires both in the
carer. ('Detachment' in any case, conveys a wrong impression of
emotional distance whereas a sense of long-term perspective, as
opposed to over-involvement emotionally, is surely what is meant.)
If I am conducting the funeral of a loved relative or great friend, it
is easy for me just to become one of the emotionally-involved
mourners – and then I can be of little help pastorally. If, on the
other hand, I remain quite emotionally aloof, seemingly without
empathy with the mourners, I am also of little help. Somehow, we
have to steer a middle course between the two, and only our
sensitivity and experience will help us to draw up the guideline.
And even then, we may err on one side or the other . . .
Later on in the day, Ken has a word to say about the chaplain.

> He was in here the other day. He seemed to think that I should
> be quite happy to be God's chosen vessel into which people
> could pour their compassion . . . That it was alright being a
> cripple because it made other folk feel good when they helped
> me.[5]

Many of us know very well how to employ strategies of avoidance
to escape involvement in the reality of pain and suffering. There are
different masks we can put on and take off when we meet people
whose situations seem intractable. We can hide behind religious

phrases like 'God's chosen vessel'; some of us can hide behind dog collars which give us at least an air of professionalism; we can hide behind the sacraments and prayers which it may be our professional privilege to administer. A religious stance can be used by anyone as a defence against costly personal involvement, against real encounters with people in despairing situations. There is an ambiguity in religion which we always need to recognize: it can open us up or shield us from God's reality.

Pastoral care, then, is a sharing of self-understanding, and an invitation to the other person to risk that sharing. Helplessness and suffering are part of the human condition, to be avoided if possible, but never at the cost of authenticity or integrity. To be ready to acknowledge and live with helplessness, it is essential for us to keep clear our vision of God in Christ and to live close to the source of our love and caring. We may not feel very expert in the ways of prayer as traditionally defined. Here, too, we may feel weak if not helpless. Again, neither success nor expertise is of much account. What matters is the attempt we make, in our own way, to keep open and warm our relationship with God, no matter how fragile it appears on occasions, and no matter how much anger we may wish on occasions to express in our prayers! Other people often sense very quickly when we have given up trying to live close to the source of our caring. Perhaps our willingness to talk about our own difficulty in praying may help those who have similar difficulties to talk more freely and honestly with us. Honesty is fundamental, not just about prayer, but about Christian faith as a whole. Relations within churches would be much more productive and healthy if we were prepared to say where we doubted, and to admit that in certain circumstances there is no easy Christian answer, even if there is one at all. But this is only to repeat that the heart of the matter is journeying towards the goal of vision rather than a 'credal package' or even a 'morality package' which we have inherited.

Christian life is an adventure, a voyage of discovery, a journey, sustained by faith and hope, towards a final and complete communion with the Love at the heart of all things.[6]

So the ambiguities in our caring, once understood and prepared for, will enable us to relax, to risk being ourselves, and give us a sense of humility which will greatly enrich that caring.

5

Counselling Insights in Pastoral Care

Counselling, it has been said, has become the greatest growth industry of the later twentieth century. Training courses multiply, and the number of counsellors and clients seems to increase week by week. Business, industry and general practitioners regularly employ counsellors, and schools have recently been added to the list. I read recently the cynical comment of the co-ordinator of a Bereavement Visitors team, who claimed that to be a counsellor these days has replaced interior decorating as a pastime. The national body for professional counsellors, the British Association for Counselling, had 1,300 members in 1977. Today it has something like 11,500, and it is estimated that at any one time something like 100,000 people are in counselling or psychotherapy.

Now, of course, reasons for this burgeoning of counselling are not hard to find. The explosion in our knowledge during this century of the inner workings of the personality, thanks to the human sciences, has led to a great concentration on and fascination with our relationships, our inner struggles and conflicts. The increasing erosion of what were considered to be ethical absolutes has led to greater personal uncertainty and a greater freedom to explore dilemmas. Further, the friendships and neighbourliness which formed a natural part of older communities no longer obtain in our more anonymous 'privatized' communities, and so make a natural trust for sharing much more difficult and sometimes impossible. (It is no accident that such sharing was found especially in the bleakness of northern industrial towns, as John Betjeman noticed in the middle of the century, redeeming and compensating for their ugliness.) Consequently, help in personal and troubled situations is increasingly sought through professional counselling, which takes the place sometimes occupied earlier by priests and ministers. (Recent research has indicated that only four out of a hundred people in trouble would seek the help today of a priest or minister. I wonder, is this because those priests and ministers are perceived as lacking in professionalism in this area, or as those who will exercise moral judgment, and not be unconditional in their caring?)

Clearly, such professional counselling has been a blessing for many thousands of people who have found in their counsellors a sensitive listening ear and a clarification of difficult issues in their lives. It has become a commonplace that any national trauma or disaster brings forth an army of such counsellors. (I was asked to be on call, ready to assist as a counsellor after the Lockerbie air disaster, but in the event there were more counsellors than were needed. I was especially relieved I wasn't called for when I heard the apocryphal story about old ladies in Lockerbie, hearing a knock at the door and drawing back the curtains to see if it were just another counsellor!) I fear that there is a real danger that, because of the mystique with which the counselling profession often surrounds itself today, as if it were some sort of arcane discipline, it will cease to be taken as seriously as it should be. Recent series of articles in the press have taken some vicious side-swipes at counselling, and tended to denigrate it in the popular mind.

Those most experienced in training counsellors have begun to see the dangers in this proliferation of professional counselling. 'Market forces will hopefully shake down the vast numbers of counsellors, as the thousands of hopefuls find less work than they imagined,' suggests Michael Jacobs, and he urges 'the expansion of free and low cost services' and 'the development of the voluntary sector'.[1] That signals the opening of a door. Those 'free and low cost services', that 'voluntary sector' includes, to my mind, those of us who are pastoral carers and who use counselling insights in our caring. It seems to me that there are three levels at which counsellors operate. The third level is of the more highly specialized sort, which we have just been considering. The first is the 'everyday level' and the second a 'basic level', which is generally exercised by those in the caring professions. We will operate sometimes more at the 'everyday level' and at other times at the more 'basic level' and from my experience, I know that those of Christian commitment to the primacy of unconditional love can acquire such insights as will both affirm them in what they are already doing and help them to be more effective still in their work.

Let us explore a little further. A characteristic definition of counselling would be that of 'a relationship through which one person seeks to help another to help himself or herself, and grow to greater maturity in the process'. So counselling is essentially a relationship, *not* a technique, or even primarily a skill, although obviously wisdom and insights can be learnt and appropriated. And if the dynamics or chemistry of the relationships are not right from the start, there is (in my view) no point in pursuing the matter further, for the essential ingredients of trust and confidence will be absent. It would be wise, then, to suggest that someone else might better be able to help. And it isn't failure on anyone's part when that happens: it is simply but humbly to recognize the situation as it really it. So no one is to blame; despite all our psychological expertise, the chemistry of relationships still remains, in large part, a mystery. Notice the little word 'seeks', seeks to help. We are not in the problem-solving business. We are dealing with persons who are muddled, irrational and emotion-ridden, and often unable, despite all the gentle probing that counselling entails, to articulate clearly their deepest feelings – or, to use the common jargon, to articulate 'where it is that they are really at'. So there is no guarantee that we shall in the end be able to help. No one can tell what the outcome of a conversation is likely to be when that conversation starts and if they can tell it simply means that there has been a deal of manipulation going on. And all manipulation is evil and contrary to the spirit of the gospel. So the word 'seeks', again, keeps us humble. Sometimes the most that we are able to achieve through the counselling process (and I do not down-grade it) is to help the other person see more clearly, and live with, a situation which is not going to go away.

And then, that other little word 'help'. Time and time again in pastoral care (as we have seen) we need to pay heed to the harmful distinction which is sometimes made between 'helper' and 'helped'. And the adoption of the helping role, as in counselling ('doing something to or for somebody'), can lead not only to patronizing but also to arrogance, quite apart from the way in which it can blind us to the reason many of us chose to be helpers in the first place – in order to be helped! (In this respect we need to avoid at all costs the possibility of people having counselling training because they see it as an escape from their own personal and pressing difficulties.)

'To help himself/herself . . . ' This is crucial. Christians are almost preconditioned to exercising moral judgment, giving 'Christian advice', almost dictating (for the other person's good, of course!) what they should do. At least, that is how Christians are perceived. None of this is ever justified in the process of counselling, if we care, as we must, about the growth of the other person to greater maturity.

Nothing closes the door to progress faster than the expression of a moral judgment, explicit or implicit, for it essentially means that we are not showing the empathy that is necessary to the counselling relationship. We are not where the other person is emotionally but standing aside, or even over and above them. It isn't in any sense that we are denying our commitment to Christian faith; in any case the other person will, in most situations, know what our stance is. And I would claim that loving empathy may in certain situations, where a lot of unpleasant material is being unleashed, demand that we temporarily suspend our own framework of values in order better to understand the forces that have led to this situation. Incidentally, could there be a better example of unconditional loving than this? It reminds me of St Paul's contention that 'Christ was innocent of sin, and yet for our sake God made him one with the sinfulness of men'.[2]

It is always, I believe, a mistake to think that unless we exercise that moral judgment the other person will not feel sufficiently guilty, and consequently will be unable to amend their lives. The sad experience of many counsellors is that most people are only too willing to judge themselves, and not just those with a religious faith. In any case, there is in the unconditional love implicit in our stance a judgment far more real and searching than any *word* of judgment we might feel called upon to make. There is an incident in the Gospels when Jesus had spoken no words of condemnation, indeed, hadn't said anything, but Peter felt himself to be judged: 'Depart from me for I am a sinful man, O Lord.' Peter saw his sinfulness simply by being in the presence of Jesus, and his unconditional love.

Nor do we give advice. The only advice which is admissible, and does not preclude the growth of the other person, is information. We will often be pressed to say 'What would you do if you were me?' and the proper answer to that question is 'I am not, nor ever will be, you and it is not for me to take responsibility for your decision or your life. I can only take responsibility for mine.' When we have, to the best of our ability, listened, empathized and understood the nature of the other person's situation, we can perhaps (if the situation is of this sort) clarify three or four choices of direction in which to go, with the corresponding advantages and disadvantages of each direction. But we cannot choose that direction for anyone else and the making of the choice will help them to take responsibility for their own lives and so grow to greater maturity. It has often happened to me that the person I was seeking to help has made a choice different from that which I would have chosen 'if I were him/her'. So be it: there may well be in the situation a hidden but powerful factor which it has not been possible for the other person to reveal and which will influence his or her choice. In this case, we affirm their decision and support them through it.

Since counselling is essentially, as we have seen, a relationship, all counselling theory would suggest that it is the personality of the counsellor which is the chief catalyst in the process of healing and growth. It is much more a matter of nurturing human qualities than of learning techniques. Competence and efficiency are obviously essential, but taken by themselves they do not make up for sensitive counselling. So what are those qualities?

It is perhaps no accident that the chief apostle of counselling, Carl Rogers, originally intended to offer himself for the ministry. He spent two years in Union Theological Seminary in New York, and acted as pastor of a small church in Vermont during the summer. The qualities he finds essential for counselling repeatedly touch Christian nerve ends. We need, he says, to be *genuine* characters who *accept* others and who show *empathy*. And following Brian Thorne, a Christian psychotherapist, I would add 'to show empathy with tenderness'. Other counselling experts since the days of Carl Rogers have used different terminologies, but do not differ from him in the nature of those essential qualities.

By *genuineness*, we mean not putting on a metaphorical or literal white coat to hide our real selves. Now that, of course, is to take a risk and make ourselves vulnerable, and it may well be that that very quality of vulnerability attracts others to approach us in the first place. Professionals who are constantly engaged in helping situations are often tempted (through sheer self-protection) to suppress more and more of themselves, to behave as they are expected to behave and to feel what they are supposed to feel. But it is just those real selves which are likely to be our richest resource. It is the genuine giving of a genuine self which is the most we have to offer. And that, it seems to me, takes us right to the heart of the way in which Jesus showed himself to those who were in need.

The second quality we nurture is *acceptance*. Carl Rogers says that he prefers the word 'prizing', the way a parent prizes a child. This doesn't mean approving all that the child does; the parent affirms the child's worth. So the counsellor affirms the worth of the other person, indicates that he or she has value, even though at that time he or she may be totally confused, and their lives such a jumble of contradictions that they feel they cannot be of use to anyone. Perhaps the giving of an hour's time simply to listen to another is to say, effectively, a great deal about that other person's worth. It may be the first occasion in their lives when they have been given the chance to know that what they feel and do matters, given the space to reflect in the company of another on their own worth. This is surely a reflection of Jesus' own words that the 'hairs of our heads are all numbered' and that 'we are of more value than many sparrows'. So the phrase which has formed a great part of the received gospel of social workers – acceptance of the client – can be seen as having its roots in the quality of acceptance displayed by Jesus and in the freedom Jesus always seems to have given to his friends to make their own decisions about their own lives.

The third quality is *empathy*. This is a quality much deeper than sympathy and the direct opposite of the common statement, uttered at arm's length, of 'I know what you're going through'. It is so hard a quality to exercise that few of us get very far along the road to empathy and yet, in my experience (and I speak as a recipient as well as – I hope – a giver) the extent to which we get along that road is the extent to which the therapy we are offering is effective. Empathy is to be inside the inner world of the other person, feeling what it is like to be him or her at that moment, lying where the patient is lying, and yet never for a moment losing our own identity. Surely again we have here a supreme illustration of 'agape', the supreme Christian virtue of unconditional love. Empathy implies the giving of one's whole attention to another person, in particular through the ministry of listening, the hardest of all arts and yet again the most therapeutic. Dietrich Bonhoeffer saw this very clearly.

> It is his work we do for our brother when we learn to listen to him. Christians, especially ministers, so often think they must always contribute something when they are in the company of others, that this is the one service they have to render. They forget that listening can be a greater service than speaking. Many people are looking for an ear that will listen. They do not find it among Christians, because these Christians are talking when they should be listening . . . In the end there is nothing left but spiritual chatter and clerical condescension arrayed in pious words.[3]

I wonder how far our stress on the words of Jesus has led to a distorted view of the way in which he must have shown himself to individuals as the most sensitive of listeners and hence the most empathic of characters? His dealing with the woman by the well in John 4 is a superb example.

The fourth quality is a quality of *tenderness*. It is a quality not easy to define and simpler to recognize, but it 'becomes a possibility at the moment when two human persons meet and are able to give way to the liberating urge to trust without anxiety'.[4] It is, says Brian Thorne, a quality which 'irradiates the total person – it is evident in voice, the eyes, the hands, the thoughts, the feelings, the beliefs, the moral stance, the attitude to things animate and inanimate, seen and unseen'.[5] And the cultivation of what Brian Thorne calls this 'at homeness' highlights still further the experience of liberation engendered by the other three qualities.

Now, assuming these qualities, making for a sound, trusting and tender relationship, experience suggests that the other person will be able to move away from their poor feeling of self-worth to a more positive attitude. Receiving such valuing and trust from another person they will then begin to love themselves a little more, and will feel sufficient self confidence both with 'where they are really at', and also with other people. Theologically, this conviction about the possibilities of change in a person comes from the belief that we are partakers of the divine nature, made in God's image, open to his spirit, loved by him and destined for glory.

Now my hope is that what we have just explored will give us increasing confidence in our involvement in informal, everyday counselling. The more highly professionalized counselling has become, and the more esoteric as a discipline, the more reticent others may have become to play a very natural part in befriending or helping those who are undergoing a crisis in their lives. And as I indicated earlier, there are many I know who, without any benefit of specific counselling training but exercising quite naturally those counselling qualities which emanate from Christian faith, have performed a valuable service for their friends and neighbours. Of course, the more psychological insights we can gain from the human sciences, the more we are able to study and reflect on our own and other peoples' experiences, the more we shall have to give. But it is easy, in pursuit of greater professionalism, to forget that however well trained and experienced we are, in the end we have only our own exposed selves to offer to another person.

Perhaps there is a considerable advantage we have over those who do full-time counselling professionally. We will be able to see our service not so much as coping with a short-term crisis in a few well-defined sessions but as a 'continuing ministry to life's normality'. We will most likely have a natural and continuing pastoral care for the person over a long period of time and will be concerned for their growth in holiness rather than falling victim to the temptation to be preoccupied with their psychological adjustment. Such 'fitting in' can never be our goal. Some of the caring professions, psychiatrists and social workers in particular, have often been criticized for exercising some sort of social control, inducing conformity to the social and political order. Oddly, the church can also make the same mistake. Goodness, as Harry Williams says, can often be confused with conformity and evil with a failure to conform. 'We have all met people who are good in the worst sense of the word. Hence, the people who rebel against the good can often be the people who bring about the realization of new forms of goodness.'[6]

In all our counselling work, we do not aim to induce conformity or even to reproduce normality. (What/who is 'normal'?) We simply help people to re-create their true selves and experience the glorious liberty of the children of God.

6

Pastoral Care at Work

Prophecy is always dangerous, and God has a habit of disposing what we propose. An old Jewish saying has it that 'if you want to make God laugh, tell him your plans!' But if and when we dare to look beyond the millennium to the future of the church – and present leadership is not strong on this point – we may see a church emerging which is not so much tied to large buildings, too expensive to maintain, and organizations which are too inflexible to change. Rather, reverting to the pattern of the first three centuries, there will be small groups meeting regularly but informally for worship and shared concerns for the community. Since the daily temptation of all small groups is to become cosy, complacent and introverted, they will need occasionally, especially at festivals, to experience worship with other groups in the larger, grander setting of a building such as a cathedral or large parish church. In this way, their vision of the wider church of God will be stretched, and unlike their usual setting, they will be able to enjoy formal worship with as much colour and beauty and panache as possible.

At present, in the Anglican Church, many churches act on the principle that their service on every Sunday is going to be a splendid occasion. It isn't. We dress up and often attempt to sing to the backs of other people psalms and parts of the communion service, which are embarrassingly difficult. But alongside that greater informality of worship, there will be far fewer professional priests, much greater lay involvement, and again, if introversion and its attendant evils are to be avoided, then ministry will be directed outwards towards the community rather than to the 'inner circle'. Still the church of the resurrection, but much more a church of the market place than a church of Victorian Gothic.

Correspondingly, emphasis in pastoral care will be more and more on places of work and secular institutions. Of course, 'representative Christian persons' – by which I mean both those ordained and lay – already exercise such care in the workplace, as we have seen, and it will become increasingly common. But my own experience in a secular television company has taught me that we must be clear about our identity and purpose.

We need, first, to relax. There is always an assumption that 'representative Christian persons' have a fixed role, a predictable agenda, and a certain way of speaking and acting as if they will have failed unless they turn a perfectly natural conversation into a somewhat strained act of witness, a sort of point-scoring for God. It is this forced and set position that we must let go. Others expect us to think and act like that. I well remember a certain incident when I was taking a seminar on our university extra-mural summer school. All the seminars joined together on one evening in the week for discussion of a general topic. In this case it was 'abortion'. And I was considerably irritated to hear a gynaecologist in the discussion saying, 'Now I know what Frank Wright would say: he would claim that . . .' And he proceeded to outline what my predictable stance on the matter would be. I rejoiced in the opportunity to prove him wrong, showing (I trust) that a Christian can think for himself and that there is only very rarely one Christian position to be adopted on any ethical question. The more predictable our stance, the less we are going to be taken seriously – and we might lose respect, on the grounds that we are not 'real people'. That stance also suggests a certain lack of confidence, almost faith, that God uses us as we are, and not because we self-consciously adopt a certain Christian perspective. Naturally, we can only do this if our lives are 'hidden with Christ in God', if, through dwelling in him, we are able to act spontaneously. Contrary to the criticism often made that Christians in secular positions simply become secular through the daily air they breathe, we need more than others perhaps to be able to draw strength from our hidden resources of contemplation and meditation, and then we can simply be ourselves. We can relax . . . We are not placed there to achieve results. Just as we saw earlier, if the church is making its demonstration of faith in the unconditional love of God, and reflecting that love to others, then it can leave the results to God. So, too, we can rid ourselves of any desire to succeed and of any anxiety about whether we are advancing the Kingdom of God by our own efforts. Perhaps we need to swim against the tide that seems to have swept through certain sections both of the church and the world at present. I mean the mania to see demonstrable and quantifiable results in what are called 'appraisals of ministry'. How can you quantify pastoral care? In this Decade of Evangelism, certain church leaders have urged congregations to double their numbers by the turn of the century. But what price quiet, steady pastoral care then? For however dedicated the carers, all their efforts will not necessarily add a single person to the faithful. Pastoral care makes no headlines, and doesn't give the church a 'higher profile' in society. Ecclesiastical careers are not usually advanced by such steady and devoted pastoral care. But for those who have eyes to see, it is its own justification.

So Christians, in secular circumstances, can be themselves. And if we are recognized by a certain quality of life that we are displaying, there will be no shortage of helping or caring situations into which we will inevitably be drawn. But we may have to wait for those chances. We may have been watched for a long time before people will have enough confidence in us to approach us about a personal situation they would like our help to unravel. I recall with a certain amount of amused satisfaction the first occasion I set foot in Granada Television as its Religious Adviser. Horrified at seeing a parson with a dog collar, one well-known presenter of the time told me in very colourful language precisely where to go. And that was at a time when Granada Television had recently won the weekend franchise – and so needed to produce religious programmes. They were very hard pressed to find not so much a committed Christian producer as one who could even basically understand the Christian vocabulary. In these circumstances, there is considerable pressure (internally from conscience, and externally from earnest colleagues) to go for a higher profile: to put notices up, to organize 'events': a carol service in the studio, a lunch-time prayer meeting, a Christian witness group. I hope it has not been cowardice, temperament, indolence or lack of commitment which have turned me away from what would have been ghetto-like activities. My own inclination, and conviction, led me to believe that my job was unselfconsciously to try and gain respect as a professional amongst professionals, to identify with others in the real situations of their lives, to be a real human being playing a loyal part in the organization, and not seeking simply to use it for Christian party ends. Again, it seems to me, we have to rid ourselves completely of that common desire to milk an organization for our own profit, however desirable the end we have in mind. Again, the *form* of Christian witness must always be consonant with the gospel – the gospel which values freedom of response, and will not countenance manipulation.

I have found that patience in gaining respect increasingly had its reward as time went on. Religious questions and difficulties could be raised quite naturally (sometimes in the lift!) and without any sense of embarrassment. In my ordained ministry of forty-seven years, I have to say that I have been asked more difficult questions about faith and its relevance to life in a television company than I have in any other sector of my ministry. And all this quite apart from the factual questions that arise in relation to programmes. (Like, 'What would a Methodist minister have worn if he had been taking a military funeral in Cawnpore in 1894?' I needed notice of this question . . .) Opportunities begin to arise, like officiating at weddings and being involved in funerals. But most of all, in being alongside those undergoing some personal dilemma: marital disharmony, children's education, parental squabbles, the aftermath of bereavement. In a company of 750 people, I could rightly be accused that in the informal manner in which I worked, lacking any formal sense of identity, I would inevitably miss someone in need who would not know me or understand my role. That, perhaps, was a price I paid. But I still felt justly rewarded (and exhausted) when, at a particularly difficult time for the company, and twenty-five years after I had joined, I was asked – and not only by the victims themselves – to counsel and sustain those who had summarily been made redundant. ('Please come and give us some hope' was the plaintive request).

Those in protected Christian situations do not often realize just how far many of those in secular fields of work, experts in their own fields, are from organized Christian faith or an understanding of that faith. So, as I hinted earlier, any attempt to introduce Christian 'events' would be seen as an alien and unwarranted intrusion, and certainly wouldn't help to establish a 'representative Christian person' in a caring role. Politely, it seems to me, he or she would be increasingly ignored.

Granting all the difficulties of prophecy, and without becoming over-dramatic, indications are that we may well be in for another dark age for Christianity and the church. Of course, there are many churches – fundamentalist, charismatic, evangelical – which are not only surviving, but apparently growing both in numbers and enthusiasm. But unless those churches have at their heart a rootedness in God's love which doesn't shrink from entering with empathy the darkest areas of peoples lives, then those churches may find themselves engulfed in shallowness and effervescence. As Father Cyprian Smith put it, 'What use is it to me to be told that I am "redeemed" or saved by Christ, when all I find within myself is a frothing cauldron of conflicting desires, fears, and insecurities?'¹ Christian faith can only come alive when all that is in that 'frothing cauldron' is addressed by proper pastoral care.

Fears for the church's survival make short cuts to commitment superficially attractive. I shudder when I pass notice boards or see car stickers with slogans like 'Jesus washes whiter' or some biblical text printed on them. How can that possibly bring a person with no understanding of faith nearer to it? Ignorance of Christian fundamentals, even the Lord's Prayer, is widespread and deep-seated in all classes of society. Something like 88%, it has been computed, don't understand a single religious word with which Christians have been familiar since their childhood. And recently, it was discovered that more people were able to recognize the sign for McDonald's, the Shell logo and the Olympic rings than they were the symbol of the cross. So the use of such words to draw people nearer is bound to be counter-productive, making only for puzzlement or blasphemy. I believe that Bonhoeffer, as he so often does, still speaks directly to our situation today when he says that there may be nothing that we can *say* about Christian faith that will have credibility. We have to find out what it means to live out the Christian life without the support of words – or at least, until as a result of action, people seeing, those words begin to make sense. 'During these years, the church has fought for self-preservation as though it were an end in itself, and has thereby lost its chance to speak a word of reconciliation to mankind and the world at large. So our traditional language must perforce become powerless and remain silent, and our Christianity today will be confined to praying for and *doing right* by our fellow men. Christian thinking, speaking and organization must be reborn out of this praying and this action.'[2] There's a powerful plea, indirectly, for the importance of pastoral care.

A deal of Christian communication consists of technical religious words shot into the air, falling on no defineable target. I have sometimes seen a sandwichboard man in pouring rain displaying biblical texts. The poor man is wet through, and the words of the text are running down the board and becoming impossible to read. In any case, no one hurrying about their business and shopping is paying any attention to his poster or to him. What a parody of Christian communication! Contrast that scene with the work of the Order founded as a result of the inspiration of the life of Charles de Foucauld who lived as a Christian presence amongst the Tuareg tribe in the Sahara Desert at the end of the last century, without making a single convert. Now members of this Order of the Little Brothers and Little Sisters of Jesus, whilst embracing traditional monastic vows of poverty, chastity and obedience, and living in small communities scattered across forty-five countries of the world, work anonymously alongside others doing the most menial of tasks. One of the brothers I met is a refuse collector and toilet cleaner in a London college. They don't try to convert or talk about religion, and they don't believe necessarily that it is they who are taking Christ to other people. Rather they feel they may be finding him wherever they are. They simply identify with other people, claiming no privileges and living out the belief in the incarnation. This means that although they would never say so they allow other people to *see* unself-conscious lives of such goodness and integrity as to make them curious about their life-style and ask questions about the reason for it. Suppose that poor man in the rain had on his sandwichboard the words, 'We love because he first loved us.'[3] They would almost certainly be meaningless to most people who pass by, even if they bothered to notice. But suppose those alongside the Little Brothers and Sisters were curious, and in effect asked, 'Why do you do what you are doing when you could live a more comfortable life?' Then they would have a ready answer, spelling out the implications of that text. And the text would make sense, because other people would have first *seen* the quality of their lives. We have to recognize that that curiosity may never be aroused, but that is to respect the freedom the gospel requires. And incidentally, contrast all this with the way in which Paul Tillich used to say that the church is marvellous at answering questions which no one is asking! And if the world is ever going to be brought nearer to seeing, understanding, and loving Christ, then first of all people have to see those gifts of humility, sharing, unselfconscious readiness to be invisible and anonymous which will challenge others in their lives, and prompt them to wonder what it is that they are missing. I say again that we are altogether too impatient to see results, to make our 'witness', and leave our mark. Neither the church nor the world today lacks noise or words. We need primarily to *see* and then the words will have meaning. 'Not everyone who says to me Lord, Lord, shall enter into the Kingdom of Heaven, but he who does the will of my Father in Heaven.'[4]

Today, modern communication gives us the chance to exercise pastoral care in ways other than face-to-face encounter. We have become accustomed for some time now to television counselling after programmes exploring social and personal problems. But at Granada, we have provided this facility after our regular series of religious programmes called Meditations, usually broadcast in Advent or Lent. In them, we have sought to bring together Christian truth and the real lives of human beings in such a way that viewers are awakened to the difference the faith dimension might make to their lives, not in simplistically dissolving at a stroke their dilemmas and sorrows, as so often tele-evangelists seek to do, but in giving them pinholes of light and hope and joy as they continue to struggle with their difficulties. Here is pastoral care informing Christian communication in such a way as to make it come alive.

But if we are going to do that we must heed Colin Morris's warning. He writes:

> By courtesy of mass media, we Christian communicators can tell the whole world about the love of God without it costing us anything more than the expenditure of a little technique and a lot of breath. It is love at a distance; at the other end of the microphone, camera or printing press. No one can tap us on the shoulder and say 'Prove it!' We are beyond reach.[5]

In other words, we must be ready to convert that love at a distance into a person-to-person exchange, allowing viewers to make their own personal response, to tell out their own particular difficulties, to be truly listened to, and given a personal reply when they write. In my view, it would almost be immoral to bring out into the open the suffering that lies just beneath the surface of so many people's lives and not allow it proper expression. So for two hours after each programme we have had a considerable number of counsellors answering the phones – and viewers can phone from any part of the country at the cost of a local call. We have also been ready to make personal contacts for viewers in confidence in their own area, either through the local church or the appropriate social service agency. I have to say that I have never been so deeply moved in my life before as I have when reading those responses after our Meditations: moved by the resources of courage that so many people display, saddened by the way in which the church often seems to have let them down pastorally and made to feel that, however inadequately we do it, this bringing together of Christian truth and the real lives of human beings is the most appropriate way forward in Christian communication. It is yet another example of the way in which pastoral care lies at the heart of Christian faith.

7

Our Relationships

In Edward Albee's play, *The Zoo Story*, the entire action takes place on two park benches on a Sunday afternoon. The two characters, Peter and Jerry, are exchanging confidences about their lives, and Jerry explains how he has unsuccessfully tried to poison his landlady's dog, and what happened the next time he saw the dog:

> 'I stopped; I looked at him; he looked at me. I think . . . I think we stayed a long time that way . . . still, stone-statue . . . just looking at one another. I looked more into his face than he looked into mine. I mean, I can concentrate longer at looking into a dog's face than a dog can concentrate at looking into mine, or into anybody else's face, for that matter. But during that twenty seconds or two hours that we looked into each other's face, we made contact. Now, here is what I had wanted to happen: I loved the dog now, and I wanted him to love me. I had tried to love, and I had tried to kill, and both had been unsuccessful by themselves. I hoped . . . and I don't really know why I expected the dog to understand anything, much less my motivations . . . I hoped that the dog would understand . . . It's just . . . it's just that . . . it's just that if you can't deal with people, you have to make a start somewhere, *with animals!*'[1]

There is an example of a poignant yet common tragedy. For some time, I lived next door to a lady who couldn't stand children or young people, but who adored her six cats as her only source of close relationships. But to live is, inescapably, to be part of a network of relationships and to belong and feel at home in such a network is a basic human need. We are born from relationship, however superficial; we are born into relationship, however inadequate our parents; we grow into relationships of various kinds with those outside our family. We need the sustaining which relationships bring if we are going to express ourselves properly as human beings. ('I need you in order to be myself.') And the question most asked about the afterlife is, 'Will I know there those I've known here?' Our caring will inevitably involve us in other peoples' relationships – and this at a time when the pattern of relationships is probably more fluid and flexible than it has ever been. So we need to understand the dynamics of relationships as best we can.

Two dangers we need to recognize from the outset: first, that of trivializing relationships and emptying the mystery of persons and the delicate thread which joins human beings together, by easy hints of the 'you need to get together' sort. 'We have to accept a darker, less fully conscious, less steadily rational image of the dynamics of the human personality,' warns Iris Murdoch.[2] Relationships, subtle and touching the deeps of human nature, cannot without damage be reduced to formulae and easy solutions. Secondly, however, and paradoxically, relationships also can be so exalted, so much talked about, that those who are not part of a happy family with many friends can come to feel that their position is much worse than it really is. We must refuse either to trivialize or over-exalt.

So what do we mean by relationship, and in particular, a healthy relationship? Ugly and unhealthy relationships are evident when we meet someone who is possessed by someone else, or eaten up with jealousy, or manipulated for ulterior motives; or worse still, when someone has become somebody's plaything or been made indispensable to another person. Healthy relationships presuppose free beings who have come to know who they are; who have come to a sense, that is, of their own particular and unique identity; and this, it must be said, will have been partly because, in their early days, they have already experienced healthy relationships. When two free beings enter into relationship with each other they are giving themselves to each other, not in order that they may dominate or be dominated by the other person, but simply because it is a good thing to be in relationship.

Whatever their abilities in other fields, relationships are the most basic way in which people can be creative. The relationship will be healthy when there is some sort of rhythm of aloneness and togetherness, when there are no feelings either of being suffocated by togetherness or, on the other hand, being deserted and made to feel lonely. It seems to me that those three conditions are crucial: a sense of identity, the ability to give oneself openly, with the recognition of all the hurt as well as the joy that may result, and a rhythm of aloneness and togetherness. I am not, of course, suggesting absolute or impossible ideals. We are dealing with people, and all of us without exception can only approximate, at best, to these conditions of a healthy relationship. But to know those conditions is not only to give us insight in our own relationships: it is also to help us discern more clearly what is wrong when we meet people who are experiencing great unhappiness because of a lack of relationships or because of inadequate relationships. We should look a little more closely at those three conditions.

A sense of identity: trouble arises when we are not genuinely free, when we're still tied by emotional bonds or even bonds of gratitude to our parents. The emphasis here is on 'tied'; it isn't that some emotional bonds shouldn't exist. If, however, we are simply looking over our shoulders to see that we are maintaining any moral or personality role that we feel is expected of us, we cannot know ourselves properly. If we are just an extension of someone else, then we have little of ourselves to give and true relationship is doomed from the start.

It is when the process of weaning from the child-parent relationship, which ordinarily happens between the age of fifteen and twenty, remains incomplete, perhaps for a long time, that human beings aren't able to detach themselves and offer themselves freely in relationship with another.

Ability to give oneself to another: to give myself is to offer all that I am, weaknesses as well as strengths, in the expectation that I shall be accepted as myself, in my readiness to be hurt, and in my willingness to suffer with the other person. Reciprocally, it means being ready to receive and understand what it is that the other is offering to you. Relationships have been characterized as being of three sorts.[3]

There are *power* relationships, when two people simply try to take from each other, and an ensuing struggle takes place, with consequent aggressive or defensive behaviour, and one inevitably becomes the loser. One partner feels better because the other feels worse. Then there are *trading* relationships, where there is neither gain nor loss on either person's part, since through compromise tacitly agreed to, both break even. It is, of course, relationship diminished in quality, since any sort of personal bargaining is bound to make a person less than fully himself. There is an absence of conflict, but that is perhaps the most that can be said. Finally, there are *loving* relationships: one person is freely available to the other – at whatever the cost. These three divisions are important because they help us to place our relationships in categories, and fix them. The truth is that most of the relationships in which we are involved will, to some extent, have something of each in them. It is the clarity which self-knowledge brings us which is important, and the constant pursuit of the third, loving relationship. You will notice how a power relationship diminishes the other partner; a trading relationship results in stalemate; but a loving relationship enhances the other partner – and that is often mutual.

Rhythm of aloneness and togetherness: If a relationship is going to be enriching, there must be periods of 'creative withdrawal' from the togetherness or intimacy that relationship entails. Only in solitude can we be fully in touch with those resources which will sustain us in relationship. It isn't only that human nature can't bear too much togetherness: it is that the quality of the relationship becomes more superficial when it is not recreated in separation. Pressure, direct or indirect, from contemporary society indicates to people that to be alone or lonely (and insufficient distinction is made between the two) is something at all costs to be avoided. Accordingly, we seek many escape-routes: not simply alcohol or tranquillisers, but breathless activity, for instance, or some noisy emotional religion, neither of which gives us time or space to face aloneness, and both of which smother the pain of aloneness which is essential to healthy growth. The rhythm of aloneness and togetherness ensures both the preservation of identity and the joy which relationship brings, and deepens its creativity. There is always more of each other to give to each other.

What, then, are the other barriers and hindrances to effective relationships? Chiefly *fear*, shown in the conscious limitations we place on ourselves to avoid the risk of coming too close to another person. It is as if we don't want to come any nearer than is absolutely necessary for the way in which we can feel safe with the part we want the other person to play, the 'limited liability' notion we have of the relationship. There are other fears, especially in struggling to make the first attempts to forge a relationship at all. Often, we fear that we shall make fools of ourselves, or not know how to 'control' ourselves. The bogy of 'control' and 'self-control' lies behind a lot of ineffectual relationships. We feel afraid that we shall make mistakes from which we shall never be able to recover or retrieve ourselves. We may lack proper self-confidence because the high expectations placed on relationship today are such common knowledge and we feel we shall never be able to 'perform' in relationships satisfactorily.

Christians believe that at the heart of the universe there is the mystery of relationship. The much-maligned doctrine of the Trinity, Father, Son, and Holy Spirit, stands for and symbolizes the distinctiveness of each Person, their equality, and their complementarity. And that circle of relationship isn't a closed circle. It isn't only the self-giving of each for and to the other, but also to the life of the world. It is a circle which is always open, and from the magnetic mysterious centre there radiates that stream of outgoing love which draws us into the circle and takes us up into the Godhead. That should say something to us about relationships which are turned in on themselves and their own preoccupations, or absorbed simply in the welfare of those involved in the relationship. (Here caution is necessary, for a relationship may still have worth and quality even if it isn't turned outwards.) There's obviously something wrong if, for instance, two people are so engrossed in their own particular activities that when they do come together, their interests are so divergent that the relationship between them is weakened. Often the pathetic discovery of retirement is that, faced with the prospect of togetherness for the first time for many years, two people discover, not the richness which is between them, but the poverty.

But two people in a healthy relationship will be able to make anyone who comes into the circle feel at home, and will see them as someone incorporated within the relationship itself.

It sounds as if I'm suggesting that given the right conditions of relationship then everything will come right. We know that it will never be like that; it is always less satisfactory and more exciting than that, at one and the same time. The truth is that our needs shift and vary, and because (albeit unconsciously) we find the satisfaction of those needs in other people, our response to those people changes as well. Other people do what we do, take from others what they need when they need it, and therefore some relationships which seem all-important one moment may seem to die a temporary death the next. It isn't a matter of conscious or deliberate deception, or letting down – though it may tragically appear so. We need to recognize that what we judge in others as fickleness or betrayal simply refers to that same fragility which, if we're honest, we're forced to recognize in ourselves. Perhaps the best friendships are those which can happen between two people who don't see a lot of each other, but enjoy each other's company when they do; and the ensuing silence doesn't spell indifference, for each knows that at the summons of a telephone call, the other will be there, available, predictable, *the same*. (Incidentally, why in Christian circles do we neglect the richness that comes from ordinary friendships?)

> Who, when great trials come,
> Nor seeks nor shuns them; but doth calmly stay,
> Till he the thing and the example weigh;
> All being brought into a summe,
> What place or person calls for, he doth pay.
>
> Whom nothing can procure,
> When the wide world runnes bias from his will
> To writhe his limbs, and share, not mend the ill.
> This is the mark-man, safe and sure,
> Who still is right, and prayes to be so still.[4]

One harmful assumption which is often made is that there must be something odd about someone who is single or without a 'steady' relationship. Loose talk, even when spiced with humour, often makes single people feel failures, or at best, second class, when they are probably being most courageous and self-actualizing by remaining as they are. The single state isn't necessarily without relationships. Being single may, and often does, free someone for a great variety of relationships with other men and women in a wide age-range. Indeed, some single people feel more 'related' than many of their friends who are apparently happily married, but locked into a domesticity which can be quite stifling. The implications of the way in which the church orders its worship and life sometimes makes it difficult for the single person, despite the fact that one in every three church members is single.

The emphasis many local churches put on family communion and family services makes many single and divorced people feel more unwanted than the church often intends. Perhaps every church needs to ask itself: to what extent are we implicitly cold-shouldering or genuinely treating with welcome and with warmth those who are single? How far are we recognizing that the single state has an intrinsic worth? Homosexual relationships continue to cause deep division within society and the church. Those of homophobic tendencies (for whatever reason) and those who determine their ethical standards simply by biblical proof-tests, condemn such relationships. But if, as recent research seems to indicate, such orientation may be of genetic origin, it would be wise to adopt a gentle approach. This would imply that this is the way they are made as God's creatures, so why should we treat them any differently from those who are 'naturally' heterosexual? We may find their orientation 'distasteful', we may not like their methods of securing recognition as 'equals', but which hetero-sexual could cast the first stone from a high moral stance? If the sexual orientation of the single person is sometimes homosexual rather than heterosexual (and this must never be tacitly assumed of single people), then it is for pastoral carers to recognize their considerable difficulties in achieving a 'stable relationship' and offer appropriate support. It is not for us, whatever our Christian or moral stance on the subject, to judge them, to set out to alter them – or, worse still, reform them!

Glorification of the family in Christian and church life can have undesirable effects. In our proper insistence on a stable family life as part of God's ordering of creation, and essential to healthy, human society, we need also to remember two other equally important truths. The first is the ambivalence with which Jesus himself seems to have regarded the family. Sara Maitland colourfully and provocatively put it like this:

> He was brought up in the original pretending family; as an adolescent he was an irresponsible runaway (and talked to strangers in public places); he deserted his ageing parents and urged his friends to do so too: mainly he hung out with an anti-social gang consisting of rebels, zealots, prostitutes and other riff-raff, and his limited domestic life centred on a household consisting of two sisters and their brother.[5]

He was prepared to admit that the family had claims on us, but asserted almost vehemently that those claims were not supreme. 'Who is my mother? Who are my brothers? Whoever does the will of God is my brother, my sister, my mother.'[6] He always seems to have laid an emphasis on obeying God as a first priority, even if it meant, as it did in his own case, leaving one's own family. Some of the harshest words he is reported to have spoken concern our duty, as disciples, to break with our own families. Then, secondly, it is easy to lose sight of the fact that families are means to ends, not ends in themselves. We are placed in families to grow as human beings, and then to outgrow those families. A parent's task is to work himself out of a job, even if he is never, whatever happens, to lose his love and care. We have to recognize the way in which suffocating family life can be destructive of personal growth, and never simply be devoted to the preservation of the family at whatever emotional cost to those who are members of it.

It looks as if by the millennium, at least four out of every five couples will co-habit before they marry, and the decreasing number of marriages seems to indicate that co-habitation is becoming the rule rather than the exception.[7] There are obviously many solid factors which account for this – not least, income tax and housing policies – but one potent and relevant factor is the poor quality of relationship which the couples have experienced in other peoples' marriages (perhaps their own parents), which makes them hesitate before embarking on such a permanent commitment. It may be honesty and integrity which suggest to them that a less binding arrangement is preferable, since it is the *quality* of relationship which matters.

Often, for instance, Christians seem to be commending the commitment of marriage simply as a commitment, without any serious regard to the wounds and scars, and what feel like the lasting hurts of one or both the two partners involved. It is as if we are simply expected to show the stiff upper lip and hold grimly on, since it is the loyalty implicit in the commitment, rather than people's needs, which seems to be of supreme importance. That is one side of the picture: the way in which commitment, simply persisted in, against all the evidence of the quality of relationship, very often diminishes those involved.

But there is an equal fact of experience to be weighed. Because our commitments are bound up with our identities as persons, and because we are who we are through the commitments we make, there is a sense of the disintegration of the self when commitments are broken – on both sides. When Thomas More, the Man for All Seasons, is urged by his daughter Margaret, to swear to the Act of Succession, and so gain his freedom, he says:

> When a man takes an oath, Meg, he's holding his own self in his hands. Like water . . . And if he opens his fingers *then* – he needn't hope to find himself again.[8]

The one who suffers the breaking of the commitment feels betrayed, and very often decides, untrue to their own generous nature, that they are not going to lay themselves open to the possibility of being betrayed and hurt again. Then, one more personality shrivels up and withers.

My view is that in matters of marital relationships (and I know it sounds trite beyond words) we need above all not to be deflected from, but always be sensitive to, a person's real needs. Whilst we will be guided by our own convictions and the values we have made our own, it will be those needs, rather than any dogmatic position of our own, which will be our chief consideration. And that will not always mean (as is often suggested) going along with the 'liberal' or easy option. It may often be a matter of helping the other person to clarify their situation and be more self-critical in it; it may be that we will be helping them to see that what will serve their own needs best will be to stay where they are, in their present relationship.

If our task as pastoral carers is not to act as marriage-guidance counsellors, still less perhaps is it to act as experts in sexual matters – even though sometimes we may have to listen to some peculiar stories! We need, I think, generally to relax about the subject. That doesn't mean that we don't take seriously the tremendous power the sexual drive asserts over our lives, and all the hurts and misunderstandings, frustrations and divisions it can cause. But it is precisely because of this that I suggest that we should relax. Admittedly, we have to have a strong sense of our own identity and self-worth to do this; but I believe that we must be ready to fly in the face of all the pressures which the conventions of society place upon us. Today, we are the victims of a sort of sexual tyranny which makes us believe that if we don't have sexual experience in a certain way, there is something wrong with us, or perhaps worse still, wrong with our partner! It's a tyranny which enforces expectations of performance on us, as if we were engaged in some sort of game or sport in which it is vitally important to win. The result is that we devalue moments of tenderness and gentleness which are as important as any correct sexual 'technique'. Perhaps the most important guideline is to see the way in which the physical expression should be appropriate to the level of the relationship between two people and the commitment implied in it. Inappropriate physical gestures quite rightly repel us: they are an invasion of our person. The arm round the shoulder, or the taking of the arm, can patronize us. To confuse levels of physical expression is to damage relationships, and hence the people involved in the relationship. Morality has a lot to do not just with prohibitions, but with the implicit integrity of the right physical expression of the right emotional level.

The psychologist Carl Gustav Jung used to say that when people brought sexual questions to him, they invariably turned out to be religious questions, and vice-versa. We need to keep the connection constantly in mind, not negatively but positively. What we believe about the love of God and so about respect for persons made in God's image, tenderness and compassion – all this is reflected in our intimate relationships. Perhaps the truth is that when we really love God, we then become better lovers!

We finally return to Albee's play, *The Zoo Story*. What about Jerry in the play, the many Jerrys who feel imprisoned, unable to break out of that high wall which circumstances, they and other people have built? No one can make relationships for another. Even when carers see so clearly that it is that lack of relationship which is causing so much pain, they are powerless to provide a remedy. Sometimes, to those who find themselves unable to make a relationship, good 'advice' makes things worse by increasing the sense of incompetence or guilt. Often the phrase 'be more outgoing' is used – as if the will weren't paralysed. (Imagine going to a social club when you don't know anybody – to *make* friends, as we say.) Exhortations to 'be more loving', often heard in church, heighten the misery – since that is precisely what their condition seems to preclude. 'You've got to make a start somewhere . . .' All we can seek to do is to be alongside Jerry as he attempts, brick by brick, to take down the walls of his own prison. It's as slow and as painful as that. And the fact that someone begins to talk about their isolation means that at least the faint beginnings of a new relationship are there – and that is the starting-point for self-acceptance and the acceptance of others.

We can also do a little self-examinaton. Are we the sort of people who are sufficiently open to, and aware of, others' needs that the more obvious barriers to relationships in *us* are removed? The good opinion we have of ourselves often deceives us. I've always thought of myself as a friendly sort of chap, at home with most people, ready to do anyone a good turn. But I had reported to me once how one of my colleagues saw me. 'Stand-offish', 'a bit arrogant', 'looks after himself' . . . Of course he was right. Unfortunately, that *is* the other side of me, and it was good for me to be brought face to face with it. It brought home to me the way in which Christian faith often unconsciously encourages us to identify only with the light, the good side of ourselves, and to deny the dark or bad side. But we are all neither 'good' nor 'bad' but both good and bad: and we need to be confronted by our shadowy side, as Jung urged, and so integrate our personalities.

The more we accept of our lives and character, the more we have attempted to face fairly and squarely both the 'nice' and 'nasty' parts of our nature, the more we shall unconsciously encourage others to come to terms with themselves and in so doing, find greater freedom. That, in turn, will give their relationships a better chance to flourish.

8

Our Three Ages

Just as every age is an age of transition, so any period can be a period of crisis in personal life. Nevertheless, there are three periods which merit especial attention, and which seem to pose particular problems: adolescence, middle age and old age. What contribution, if any, can we make towards their resolution?

Adolescence

I am diffident about trying to write authoritatively about adolescence, since I am a long way past it personally, and I don't have the same continual contact with young people that I used to have. But I am still convinced that we should go on seeking to understand and respond to the needs of young people, whatever age we are, at a time when even parents and many others write them off as being 'quite impossible'. And compared with thirty or forty years ago, the church, as I observe it, largely ignores young people, and they ignore, or even despise, the church as being out of touch and totally irrelevant to their lives.

We need to recognize how many adolescents suffer mentally and emotionally in what is a period of bewildering physical change and considerable personal and social pressures. Older people seem to find it hard to have any compassion towards the noisy, awkward, rebellious, rude, volatile creatures that adolescents often are. (We find it difficult to remember that four or five years earlier, we were seeing them as delightful little boys and girls.) Their earlier physical maturing fits uneasily with a lack of experience of life and a world of confused moral values. Increasing numbers come from broken homes and single-parent families, and haven't the experience of a healthy and balanced family life. (A university admissions tutor said recently that students coming from a stable family background are now very much the exception.) They are an easy target for much of the advertising world since in some cases (the unemployed excepted) their spending power on non-essentials is considerable. They have great anxieties about finding a job, or anything like a fixed career structure. Above all, they have inherited a world which seems to offer little hope of global stability in the future, and in which inequalities abound to make the rich people and countries more prosperous, and the poor more poverty stricken. This is the world in which they are to make their mark and develop a life that is worth living. (And 'making their mark' is vital to them, echoing all that we saw earlier about the importance of a feeling of self worth.) The severe pressures on them to conform to fashion, be it in clothes, music or general life-style, leave many lonely and isolated; and just at the stage when they have begun to 'see through' their parents, they often have no one to whom to turn for encouragement.

It is here, I believe, that we may have something to offer to adolescents. Of course, until we can begin to feel their world as they feel it (and that is extremely hard for those of us who are products of a very different age), we cannot be of much help to them. Our natural inclination is to 'advise' them or, worse still, be censorious about their way of life: that widens the generation gap rather than bridges it, and it's sad to see how on the whole we older people blame the younger for the existence of that gap at all. Once we begin to get under their skin, we can appreciate many of their gifts and qualities: their honesty (very painful to see at times, for it illuminates our own hypocrisies), their care for justice, and often, their generosity. Few things are more impressive, because confidence in this respect is extremely hard won, than a relationship between an older person and an adolescent in which the adolescent is able to talk freely, even about intimate matters, without feeling that he or she is going to be judged and thought less of for so doing. This is rare, but it is possible, and I have seen it happen in the context of normal parish life. I recall the way in which one lady, whom you would recognize as having all the characteristics of the middle class, got to know well two rough lads from bad homes, and acted as confidante to them in their very different circumstances. True, there was an occasion for meeting: the lady dispersed Coca Cola three times a week in the lads' club, to which the boys belonged. And granted all our present difficulties, surely a priority for any church should be the possibility of such a provision where older people and younger people can really meet (and the really is important), so that out of that meeting over a period of time, and quite spontaneously, friendships can grow and, when it is necessary, adolescents can share their difficulties with at least one other person. One valuable way of doing this is through honest discussion of what we believe, and why; and what difference such beliefs make in our experience of life.

This isn't as tame and trite as it appears. It seems to me that adolescents have three needs in particular. First, they are searching to discover who they are, trying to reconcile attitudes and ideas they have imbibed from their own family background with those they have come up against in the wider world, and so, of knowing where they stand. Secondly, they are very often feeling great confusion and sometimes guilt about sexual matters and about their own attitude to people and life in general. And thirdly, they are looking for a framework of values in which to live their lives, and give them landmarks for the future. In all these needs, we can help through our unconditional friendship. One of the ways in which we will help will be in the gentle but piercing asking of questions about attitudes. Adolescents are often totally dogmatic or idealistic in their views. (I recall expecting the world to be completely saved by socialism and pacifism when I was eighteen.) It is important, however, not to settle for the old adage which simply suggests to young people, as it comes over to them with all the cynicism of age, 'You'll grow out of it!' Questioning is helping them to see that the matter may be more complicated than at first they thought, and so needing further depth of investigation. From an early age, we take our values unconsciously from those whom we come to admire rather than from any attempt on the part of others to teach us directly. So we can relax, let be. Our friendship, and what they see in us in unguarded moments, will be a source of moral values for them – for better or for worse!

In this way, we will be unconsciously demonstrating our own commitment to Christian faith and, incidentally, helping the adolescent in this vital matter of commitment.

We all know how some religious cults operating mainly in the States, but increasing over here, have caused much distress to parents of adolescents, who have seen their children, as it were, taken into slavery, by the wholesale irrational commitments such cults demand. Two apparently contradictory features seem to be marks of the moral climate in which we live. One is the seemingly increasing willingness on the part of often intelligent young people to commit themselves to such fanatical sects: the commitment is total to the point of dehumanization. The other feature is the strong temptation to lead lives where any commitment is seen to be cramping and restricting, damaging to any possibility of a fulfilled and enjoyable life. Underlying this is the notion that to own no final loyalties, no binding commitment, is the only sure road to fulfilment. (Here perhaps it should be remembered that to refuse commitment is still in one sense to be committed – to neutrality.) Adolescents in extreme sects are said to come in the main from affluent and fairly privileged homes where it is possible to buy your way out of or into everything. Is the impetus to commitment in such cases something to do with the way in which they recognize the emptiness which marks the life in which all commitments are seen to be infantile, regressive and imprisoning? They perhaps see that hollowness for what it is worth. Of course, all this is only to underline the importance of our own commitment, which in its turn radically affects other people. It might even make us ask the question, 'To whom or what are we committed?' at greater depth.

I like the analogy I once came across, comparing the world of the adolescent to a football field. He must have plenty of space to move in, kick the ball about, so to speak, experiment in attack and defence, prove himself; but there must also be a clearly defined pitch, with well-marked sidelines; there must be not only a first-aid helper ready with his sponge, but a referee who will be there in the background, ready to blow his whistle as little as possible. It is the privilege of pastoral carers to be both first-aid person and referee! There perhaps the analogy breaks down a little: the pastoral carer isn't only impartial, he or she is on the side of the adolescent as well.

Middle Age

The recognition that middle age often represents a time of personal crisis is fairly recent. Previously, it was assumed that only the early and latter stages of life needed particular concentration: in the period between, you just muddled through! Now we see much more clearly that the vague feelings of dissatisfaction with life which seem to accumulate especially between the ages of thirty-five and fifty-five bring on problems which are as acute as those of any other age group, but which have received much less sympathetic attention.

Social factors at present, such as unemployment and redundancy, have immeasurably exacerbated features already at work nurturing tension and unhappiness. For middle age is primarily a slow arriving at a moment of truth. It is the point at which we are able to look both backwards and forwards, and often not to like what we see. Looking back, we see that the qualities and difficulties we recognized in ourselves at an earlier stage in life still persist, and may have hardened; and that we carry around with us problems from long ago which are still unresolved. We are the same as we were – only more so. Worse still, perhaps, we begin to see those same sad qualities reproduced in our children. We see, too, that the hopes and ambitions we entertained at an earlier stage in life are unfulfilled. As we peer into the future, there may seem little likelihood either that we shall be able to change, or that we shall ever realize those ambitions. We seem so stuck in our frustrations that we can become an easy victim of disillusionment and cynicism. Increasing physical limitations remind us that old age is round the corner. Death has ceased just to be a remote possibility which happens to other people, but begins to assume a real shape for us, and the incidence of road accidents and coronary thromboses increasingly fill it out.

Of course, a lot of our frustration is to do with unrealistic expectations that we have harboured or that have been fostered in us by social factors, and in particular by mass media. The false and unreal dogma that we all deserve a higher standard of living year by year is matched maritally, as we have seen, by too high a degree of expectation as to what relationship can offer and achieve; and further, that instant remedies, such as divorce, can effect a change for the better. Unspoken-of failure is a constant feature of middle age. In career terms, if you have gone as far as you can go by the age of forty, you tend to reckon yourself as a failure; if, on the other hand, you are a success in the world's terminology, you perhaps despise that success, and see how little inner peace it brings. In both cases, the middle-aged person seems to be the loser.

Once we have come to terms ourselves with our own middle age, we have, I believe, something to offer to those who seem beset with its difficulties and see few, if any, of its opportunities and advantages. The fact that, biologically, we are superfluous after the age of forty, that we have reproduced ourselves in our nuclear families, seems to me extremely symbolic. It is no coincidence that so many women between the ages of thirty-eight and forty (and even older now) either have or want to have one last child; otherwise, they feel, they would face life without a clear role. Increasingly our working lives are shorter and shorter as longevity increases and automation takes over, and this, too, shifts the emphasis from our significance as useful human beings to our own intrinsic worth, a shift we have already explored. In other words, middle age can be the point at which we can become sufficiently detached, sufficiently removed from attachment to false values that we can begin to appreciate human life for what it is, now that we can understand its proper limitations.

Perhaps our understanding of limitations is the key to middle-age health – and beyond. Our growth as human beings and the growth of civilization seem to depend on rebellion against limits in life. In his massive *Study of History*, Arnold Toynbee concluded from his survey of twenty-seven civilizations that civilization started to flourish when people had the right amount (not too many, not too few) of physical limitations to struggle against, and were able to make the right response to a reasonable challenge. The same is true of much creative work, and certainly of the visual arts. The psycho-analyst Rollo May tells the story[1] of how Duke Ellington explained that since his trumpet player could reach certain notes beautifully, but not other notes, and the same with his trombonist, he had to write his music within those limits. 'It's good to have limits,' he remarked. Rollo May went on to say that Michelangelo's writhing slaves, Van Gogh's twisting cypress trees and Cezanne's yellow-green land-scapes of southern France are all great works of art, because whilst they have spontaneity, they also have that mature quality which comes from the absorption of tension, and that, in turn, is the result of the artist's successful struggle with and against limits.

So limits are valuable, and the struggle against them healthy and conducive to our growth. To keep on trying to push back bit by bit the limits in our lives is essential; the saddest people are those who have nothing to fight for and against. But that is only half the story. Futile struggle against certain inescapable limits can only produce frustration and bitterness; acceptance of those limits and working within them, on the other hand, can bring a deal of satisfaction and happiness. We all know some people who, having accepted the inescapable limitation of some physical handicap like deafness, seem to transcend the limitation because of their acceptance of it. One of the most contented people I've known, a cousin of mine, deaf from birth, spent his life helping other deaf people with their problems. Even so, none of us ever fully transcends our limitations, especially those placed upon us by our heredity and early upbring-ing; we may try to deny them, we may sometimes use them to good advantage, but the effects of them never finally leave us. And when we remember that Jesus was born of poorish parents in a crowded little house in a small, backward, powerless nation right on the circumference of the Roman Empire, we can see clearly that it isn't outward circumstances in our lives which are totally conditioning. What matters more is our self-knowledge and self-acceptance: our self-knowledge which allows us to accept ourselves, whatever our gifts or lack of them. We sometimes oscillate between two poles: on the one hand, of thinking that it's only other people who have limitations and not us, and on the other, that of thinking that because we're lazy and unimaginative, we have limitations which can never be overcome. Many of the tragedies in world history have been caused by those of the first sort, men and women who have considered themselves sovereign or infallible or almighty; much of the real encouragement in world history has come from those who have triumphed over what at first sight seemed like paralysing limitations.

Now world history may seem some way away from the crises of our own lives in middle age. But middle age is above all the point in our lives when to see limitations clearly for what they are is essential to stability and happiness, then and thereafter. So it may well be helpful for a middle-aged person to confide in someone whose candour and honesty will help them to discern between the limitations we impose on ourselves and those limitations which are ours because that is how God made us, and which we simply have to accept. Our role, then, here and often elsewhere, is that of being a personal aid to self-knowledge, one who helps others pray that prayer of Reinhold Niebuhr, the theologian, with real meaning: 'God grant us the serenity to accept what cannot be changed, the courage to change what can be changed, and the wisdom to know the difference.'

Old Age

Those over the age of sixty-five will represent just over 15% of the population by the end of the century, and the gap between their obvious needs and the ability of the welfare organizations to supply them is increasing all the time. State provision of institutional care for those unable any longer to look after themselves is becoming increasingly difficult. We need to use our influence to develop radical thinking about how society is going to cope with the elderly in the next two decades. In 1900, the average life span in England was forty-eight; today it is nearer seventy-six. And healthier lives mean that equal consideration must be given to the elderly as to the rest.

It seems to me that it is in the matter of attitudes that, as pastoral carers, we can best make our particular contribution to the welfare of the elderly. Even in some of the best run clubs for older people, the impression sometimes given is that older people are to be treated as children and patronized, that they may expect to receive all but have little to give. Older people can obviously be awkward and cantanker-ous: unlovely characteristics displayed earlier in life can become exaggerated in later life. But we do not begin to tap the wisdom and the life older people still have to offer. Given sufficient leisure and patience on the part of the listener, many of them have fascinating stories to tell about their earlier lives. Ronald Blythe's book *The View in Winter*² is just such a collection of fascinating stories of people from very different backgrounds, and makes us realize how gloomily we are preoccupied with the difficulties of old age rather than the possibilities.

Our present cult of youth has made us value far too little the contribution older people can make, given sufficient encouragement, to our common lives. The familiar caricature of an old grandmother sitting in the corner 'being quiet and not interfering' is redolent of an attitude we like to foster, but even that is too hopeful, since today it is more likely that grandmother will be removed from the family, and put in an institution of some kind. Older people feel they have to fight continually for their dignity, their self-respect, their right to be taken seriously; and the paradox is that the better we provide for them in material ways, the greater that fight becomes. Apart from physical infirmity, they have the additional difficulty of seeing their contemporaries and friends depart this life, one by one: for them, bereavement is seemingly a constant process, and increasing loneliness a real threat, which is often unadmitted because of their pride. All this means that self-esteem and self-worth, which is of the essence of humanity at whatever stage in life, needs constantly to be nurtured. At the emotional and spiritual level, older people are, of course, threatened very much by change, and the speed of change in every sphere of their lives now is completely different from what it was when they were younger. How often is there anyone who really has the time and patience to talk through with them the effect that the speed of change is having on their inner lives?

In the pre-retirement course on which I teach, I constantly urge members to find some older person living alone and close to them whom they might visit (often, just to listen) on a regular basis. I stress 'regular' because especially if you're housebound, and look forward to a particular point at which someone comes to see you, then the sense of being let down and disappointed is bitter if it doesn't happen and you're not warned in advance. By definition, those most on their own and who need to be 'discovered', since they are less obvious, are most in need of such visitation, and churches are best placed in local areas to locate them.

There are several jobs which older housebound people can do for the church. House groups can sometimes meet (even though in some places there may be practical difficulties) in the homes of older people, to ensure that they are still able to participate. Above all, perhaps, older people, no longer able to be physically active or able to take much part in social activities within the local church, feel privileged to be asked to intercede regularly for one or two people. It isn't necessary that they know much about the circumstances of those for whom they intercede, although clearly the more links that can be made which fill out their imagination, the better. We haven't begun to explore very far yet the latent spirituality in older people who are housebound, and who have the leisure and the space denied to those who are younger. The development of such spirituality in older people presupposes that some of us will feel that we have the capability and confidence to help here – and there is no need to think that it should simply be the preserve of the clergy or minister. The strengthening of our own lives of prayer can come from sharing with one another our own insights and our own difficulties as much as from formal instruction (if not more so). Courses of formal instruction about prayer rarely seem to help some people who actually need to be strengthened in their own individual approach. We need to become as natural in our approach to prayer as we are, for instance, to Meals-on-Wheels! This prayer dimension is an essential feature of the way in which we pastorally care for other people. If prayer is

> The Christian's vital breath,
> The Christian's native air

as James Montgomery's hymn puts it, we can't fulfil our responsibility without being ready to help here. We're not called upon to be very good at it (if we were, I shouldn't have the temerity to write about it at all); we are to recognize its basic importance, and to share what little we know with others, even if we ourselves still have to say, with the last line of the hymn,

Lord, teach us how to pray.

9

Our Grey Areas

Boring, boring, boring . . . To some people, part of the unattractive-
ness of the church lies in its sameness. They complain that, unless
you're a member of a charismatic church, there's little to be excited
about, hardly anything fresh which takes you out of the monotonous-
services routine. 'In the church,' as an ecclesiastical historian put it,
'it is always Monday, God's washing day, wiping away tears and
washing away sins.' But there, if only we could see it, is its real glory;
and what is true of the church is also true of pastoral care. It will be
but rarely that we're involved in anything dramatic or exciting. The
more exotic and complex difficulties like the increasing drug abuse
among young people or alcoholism are agendas for the experts, even
if there is considerable support we can offer to those closest to the
victims themselves. Our pastoral care will largely be taken up with
the unromantic, grey areas of life, those areas where there may not
seem to be anything violently wrong, but where people feel anxious
or empty, depressed or guilt-ridden; or where perhaps they may just
be suffering from middle-age 'blues'. So let us explore these areas in
turn.

Anxiety

Freud made an important distinction between normal and neurotic
anxiety. Normal fear is that common to us all, which is anticipation of
some future event, perhaps a crucial interview, a family confrontation or a surgical operation. Such fears can work to our advantage,
for they can prepare us to cope with the practicalities of what is likely
to happen – provided, of course, that we are not irrationally
overwhelmed by these fears, and provided that we can find someone

with whom to work through that preparation. It is here that our role is crucial. Our understandable first reaction is to confront the fear, and say that it shouldn't exist. We use comforting words about there being nothing to worry about, that many people have gone through the experience safely, and that in a few weeks' time our anxious friend will look back and wonder what all the fuss was about. We may go further and add a biblical quotation about 'the everlasting arms'. But you can't deny the reality of fear so easily. If it's true that it can have a positive value, then it lies in the way in which, together, the entire process which the fear inspires may be explored in detail beforehand, and then there can be a looking forward which doesn't have concealed within it unknown terrors. I have often found that anxious people can be helped to look at a range of possible repercussions, even 'the worst that could happen'. They then relax when they find that it is actually within their powers to cope. It may be that especially in those cases where an operation is to be faced, we can discover more information about it which the patient hasn't been able or doesn't want to find, and work through the information with him or her. That will give confidence, not only in us, but in the event itself, for the normal fear (which never leaves us) is fear of the unknown.

Some normal anxiety, then, can be used constructively in order to prepare realistically for what lies ahead. All of us are anxious at certain times, but most of us manage. However, much anxiety which we encounter will not be of this normal sort, but rather that which is neurotic. In this case, anxiety isn't necessarily related to the anticipation of a particular event, nor is it just a passing mood. Rather, it is like an unwelcome visitor who comes unannounced, and never leaves. There is a general feeling of foreboding, that something terrifying lies just round the corner, a perpetual sense of unease which sometimes reflects itself in physical symptoms. To other people, the anxieties may seem unreal, as if the person were bluffing – or simply weak-kneed – and we may find it difficult to be patient with them. I recall the number of times people have said to me 'I could shake him', about someone in this state, and frequently we may feel moved to reach a judgment about the selfish obsession of the person concerned, especially when compared with the weight of starvation, homelessness, persecution and fatal illnesses which press on so many in the world. But in my experience, if we urge comparisons, make exhortations, or even give explanations, we drive them further into their misery, and make them run away from those of us who genuinely seek to help. We simply reinforce their feelings of guilt and inadequacy for being like this in the first place. Sometimes, of course, it is we who can't stand being in the presence of such gloom, feeling so helpless. It is often difficult to discern 'who is doing what to whom' in situations like this! And despite our helplessness, 'standing by' people in their state of neurotic anxiety, trying to go at their pace, rather than forcing them to accept the pace we'd like to move them to, is the most we can do. It is not for us to seek to cure them, however valuable the personal support we offer them, which in itself is therapeutic. We may have to urge them to seek both temporary alleviation, through tranquillizing drugs, and expert long-term psychiatric help. Incidentally, one difficulty we shall often encounter is the prejudice against receiving help from psychiatrists, which partly stems from the stigma attached to any suggestion of mental illness. But psychiatrists are our allies, potential liberators of the human spirit. No more than any other profession are they infallible and, as many of them would be the first to admit, there is a lot yet to be learnt about the human psyche and its health. That means that, like the rest of us, they may be tempted by some short-cut answer that can be disastrously wrong in some cases, and they can sometimes fail to be able to help. But we shouldn't hesitate in suggesting that those who seem to need treatment should see a psychiatrist, whilst at the same time helping them to see that we seek to refer them not to ease our trouble but theirs, and that in no sense are they being abandoned.

Emptiness

An increasingly common experience, in my view, and typical of the 'grey areas of life', is that feeling of coldness, or emptiness at the centre. It is as if for some people, life has lost its heart and point. It isn't that they're ill, or facing trying circumstances; indeed, in many cases, it often seems to be those for whom life is comfortable and without any major worries to whom this happens. Even the worthwhileness of religious faith, which perhaps they have never up to this point questioned, seems to desert them. Life becomes mechanical, almost a matter of shadow boxing. When this has happened to people I know, I've often felt that it is because of someone, something, some one event which has caused them to stop and pause, and then reflect; not necessarily a crisis, or even something of which they've been very conscious. It is as if they've been on a fast-moving train with scenery flashing past at great speed, and the momentum of the journey has borne them along. Now the train has stopped. The various activities of life, getting on at work, bringing up a family, arranging the busy-ness of life, have so far given sufficient momentum to living; but now these are all looked at with some detachment. It is as though people going through this experience have never developed a still, rich centre which holds when all the activities at the circumference stop, since the centre is not dependent on those activities, but exists of itself.

Situations like this are not patent of a quick or a uniform solution. People need to be helped to discover within themselves the soil in which that still centre may grow. There's little doubt in my mind that the soil exists in us all, but it is fed and watered by different means, and it will be a slow growth. Someone I know was transformed, she felt, by opening her eyes and really looking for the first time at the shapes and colours in the local park. She felt a great peace and a flooding back of life at the centre as she contemplated the pattern of bare trees and the sun playing through them on to the lake below. For others it will be listening, rather than looking, and perhaps to that music which is the 'soul of man speaking to the soul of man'. Both looking and listening are ways through which we can be taken out of ourselves and immersed in a world which, in a curious way, is beyond us and part of us at the same time. Another means of nourishment is through the experience of open, loving and relaxed relationships to be found in some groups and, we trust, in many groups within the church. Here it must be stressed that the nourishment is indirect. Any attempt directly to nourish is analogous to force-feeding, and is bound to fail. We belong, simply because it is good to belong, and we enjoy other people, not because we're looking for a result of our belonging. That would be fatal, and would spoil the relationships themselves. One other possibility is that of taking on a small piece of voluntary work, such as visiting regularly one older person. Again, it is the business of being taken out of the same circumstances which have produced the deadness of spirit, the emptiness inside.

Of course, the situation may bring to the minds of some of us that well-known quotation from St Augustine that we are made for God himself, and that our hearts are restless until they rest in him. That is a profound truth, and we may feel that we have sometimes, through our own pain and heart-searching, stumbled on the truth of it for ourselves. But like all profound truths, we need to grow into it: it cannot be presented as a panacea or instant remedy for that emptiness, which may have much to do with feelings about the unreality of God, and his absence. It may be that not only has there been death of worthwhileness elsewhere, but the death of God, too. What then? I don't believe that the means of resolution are any different from that of which we have already spoken. Truly to look, listen, love and care is to touch the hem of God's garment, even if we never look up and make the connection between the garment and the wearer. Some in time may look up, and perhaps come to see, dimly at first, his face, his gaze, his love. I have often found that line from Newman's hymn, 'And in the depths be praise', comforting and illuminating. It suggests that to those for whom all the traditional imagery of God has died, he may still be found in the depths of being, even deeper than the worst anxieties. Such reassurance is often to be found in the Psalms, a treasury of grace which captures every mood and phase of human existence.

Our job as carers is gently to make such suggestions as seem most likely to be helpful to the person concerned, and so far as we can, to share the experience with them. If it is in looking and listening, it will be in silence, and silence shared can again powerfully point to that still rich centre for which we all seek. Shared silence is something which takes great courage to risk with someone, but it is often most therapeutic. The quiet contrast to that feverish activity which has led to the feeling of emptiness is striking.

Failure

Allied to this feeling of emptiness is the feeling many of us have that we are failures as human beings. The very phrase is a contradiction in itself. It implies that we can be successful as human beings. Take two extremes as examples. We can be successful, first, at many things: in getting to the top in our careers, in acquiring much wealth, in gaining popularity. But none of these 'successes' necessarily means that we have become mature human beings in the process, or achieved the goal towards which all humanity strives; the only way, that is, in which the word 'success' is applicable to human beings. Then, at the other end of the scale, when we seem to fail at everything we turn our hand to, and we slip tragically easily from 'failing at' to 'being failures', we may have been able to begin to work through our failures, and see them as part of the maturing process – and that is success! After all, Christian faith has always known about defeat turned into victory, and tragedy becoming the source of hope.

This, it seems to me, is the attitude with which we must approach those who only see themselves as failures. Perhaps it's worth reflecting that if they have arrived at this stage of self-awareness, it is a stage further on than those who have been sheltering for years behind something which the psychologist calls the 'belonging-identity' (whether it be possessions, family or even their beautiful dog!) to hide the truth of their 'failure' from themselves, to prevent them from becoming self-aware. To be able to face the truth about our own feelings without that sort of self-defensive prop is often hard won, but it is great gain, and the first stage towards recovery. And whilst I profoundly believe what I have just been saying about 'success' and 'failure' as human beings, and indeed see it to be one of the keys to a more humane and caring society, we have to recognize the great pressures on all of us to be 'successful'. Despite the reaction and rebellion amongst many young people, the aims, standards and values of what has been called the 'achieving society', even from junior school age, are still much with us. We value highly the skills required for success, whether it is the achievement of educational grades or adequate sexual performance. Even the church is infected: isn't the successful church seen as that which simply has a large congregation, flourishing activities, and a big financial turnover?

However, once we begin to see that we are here not to achieve success, but to be human and mature, we are released from a good deal of pretence and make-believe. I have a particular aversion to those annual photocopied letters which purport to give you all news of the family over the past year. It isn't, I hope, that I am uninterested in the welfare of my friends and their children; it is that somehow, they seem to be so unreal in the promotions they've been given or number of 'O' or 'A' levels their children have acquired. Where are the failures we all have and know? Doesn't friendship actually mean that you can talk about them as well – with confidence? A clerical friend of mine once did a spoof letter in which he drew attention to 'grandmother having piles, John going on pot and Diana becoming pregnant at the age of sixteen'. Why aren't they ever like that? We needn't pretend that our marriages are the supremest of supreme successes, or that our children are the sparkling success they might be. We are all failures to some extent; what matters is the quality of love that is born out of our failure to be as good as we ought to be, as much as from being good itself. And when we see that, we have in a sense ceased to be failures, and ceased simply to see ourselves as failures.

Paradoxically, too (and here we touch time and time again the heart of pastoral care), it is often our failure to know how to help, our helplessness, our simple identification with others in their weakness and failure, that most helps other people – provided that we do not shirk the failure, or pretend that it isn't there. That is both demanding and liberating at one and the same time.

Guilt

There is one characteristic that is common to us all, very little talked about, and most deeply felt. I mean, of course, our guilt feelings. I recall an agony columnist saying that the great majority of her letter writers were plagued with guilt – about children, husbands, wives, parents, about their very existence – and I recall our televised Meditation centred on guilt where the average length of call was thirty-five minutes, and the lines were jammed. In my experience, guilt, spoken or unspoken, lies at the root of most situations presented by those who come for counselling.

As with anxiety, guilt feelings have a positive and useful function. We feel guilty when we allow what we want to do to take the place of what we feel we ought to do. And of course, if that didn't happen, if we always did what we wanted and never felt guilty, we should have a more desperate situation still. Guilt feelings can make us responsible in our relationships with other people and prompt us to be reconciled with those we've hurt by our own thoughtlessness or carelessness.

But most guilt isn't like that: it's much more irrational. One lady said in all seriousness to me, 'I feel guilty because I don't seem to have anything to feel guilty about!' There was another lady I used to meet most mornings as she made her way to the station and I made mine to church. For months as we passed each other we just said, 'Good morning'; and then one day she stopped me and said, 'I wish I didn't meet you. All you do is smile and pass the time of day, and I always feel so guilty!' She then began to tell me how she knew she ought to go to church, but didn't – for a host of good reasons, as it turned out. That reminded me how in the church we can get people to do things they wouldn't otherwise do through manipulating their guilt feelings; indeed, you can get people to do almost anything if you make them feel guilty enough about what they're enjoying at present. That is a very dangerous temptation, and we can always persuade ourselves that we're doing it for the best of reasons.

Of course, the real role of the church is to release people from their guilt, not increase it. The mechanics of release through the appointed ways of confession and absolution, formally and inform-ally, still exist, and are helpful to many. But while statistics are obviously impossible to arrive at, it seems as if the practice of formal confession has declined for quite complex reasons. They stem, I believe, first from the way in which confession of our personal sins seems a private luxury by comparison with our corporate responsibi-lity for the hunger, cruelty and violence which disfigure the world. Secondly, there is a loss of confidence, generally, in what the church provides for our good, because of its own confusions. The subject of confession has been so bedevilled by ecclesiastical wranglings and prejudices that the therapeutic values of what is being offered is inevitably lost. Thirdly, there is the question as to whether ordained parsons are the right people to understand, or whether they are too insulated from 'real life'. This is often not true at all, but it is a general perception. Finally, there is often a total rejection of the old categories and definitions of sin, and an awareness that if you are to admit to the roots of what is wrong, it takes far more both in time and in the language of nuance and subtlety than petty lists of the old-fashioned sort. My adolescence was haunted by the questions posed in the 'little red book' I was given at my confirmation about whether I had had 'naughty thoughts'(!) since my last communion – or, worse still, whether I had been in a 'Nonconformist chapel'!

There will always be those who don't or can't use the means of the confessional. How can we help them? Many of us hug our guilt to ourselves because we're deeply afraid that if we shared it with others they'd cease to have as good an impression of us, or even cease to love us. Parish priests find this to be true of parishioners who sometimes prefer to go to confession elsewhere; the truth is that such are not thought any less of, but rather more. I have heard counsellors operating in the secular field argue that what they lack is some kind of sacramental act, whereby those whom they have helped are reintegrated into ordinary relationships and shown outwardly that whatever has been the nature of their 'confession', the counsellor's respect for them as individuals is not diminished. An arm round the shoulder scarcely seems adequate.

All this argues that if we're to help other people, we must be the sort of people who can inspire such confidence that they're able to feel that they can tell their full story to us. It isn't that we must give an impression of perfection, or near perfection, but rather that we should reveal ourselves, too, as people who have struggled, or are struggling, with matters unresolved in our own lives. It will be our attempt to be unconditional, people whose lives don't depend on respectability, or on the other person's always doing what is right, combined with an openness and receptivity which will draw people out, reassured by the knowledge that our love will stay, whatever it is that the other person has to tell us. I am not suggesting that we should encourage others to parade their guilt, or wallow in it: few things are more conducive to boredom in the listener and to self-pity in the teller. I am indicating that we need to be those who encourage the cause of guilt to be brought out into the open, and allow others to share their guilt with us. That sort of release, that draining away of inner poison, is desperately important.

Depression

Anxiety (of both sorts) and emptiness, however difficult to live with, are states you might describe as being of partial eclipse. By contrast, the real state of depression, by which I don't mean a fluctuation of mood which includes feeling just a little under the weather, is a state of almost total eclipse. Confusion with the mood of feeling slightly depressed has meant that depression hasn't been understood for the total experience of blackness that it represents, and the result has been that the patient's suffering (I say patient, for depression in this sense is an illness) hasn't been taken as seriously as it might have been. Depression is a state of feeling utterly alone, on the edge of a black abyss, from which you can find no resources within you or without to organize an escape.

It has become common to talk of two types of depression – endogenous, which has its roots in the patient's personality or in his chemical balance or imbalance; and reactive, which arises as reaction to some external event, like the personal loss of a relative or friend or disappointment in promotion. This distinction is not exact, and recent research seems to indicate that depression is measurable along a scale of intensity, the differences relating to the strength of the depression rather than to its particular kind. Now clearly, since depression is an illness, expert medical and psychiatric help is necessary: Gerald Priestland, in describing his own depression (which needed a captial 'D'), said that he thanked God for modern drugs and psychiatry, and many of us have evidence of the way in which tranquillizing drugs have been a godsend (in the literal sense) to those suffering from depression. At the same time, we can't begin to cope with ourselves and with life generally by means of drugs, and continued use of drugs can prevent rather than help a person to come to terms with his own situation, because it can blur his sensitivity. It has recently been discovered that when two comparable groups of animals are subjected to experimental stress, those which are given no treatment develop a natural tolerance towards stress, and begin to adjust. On the other hand, those given anti- anxiety drugs do not develop this natural tolerance, and in the end are worse off, because they are locked into the anxiety state. This seems to indicate that drugs can drive human victims deeper into anxiety and dependence.

In addition to expert psychiatric help, or in the absence of it, there is a considerable contribution, therefore, which relatives and lay carers have to make to the welfare of a depressive. In my experience, it is the lack of any sense of self-worth which is his or her dominant characteristic, and it is often extremely wearisome for the one who stands by to have repeated over and over again the catalogue of feelings of hopelessness, misery, failure, despair and self-disgust. But we have to accept that the victim is suffering real pain, and the expressions of self-disgust do not necessarily come out of self-pity but out of great inner anguish. And the hardest part is the business of going on soaking up these painful feelings without trying to stop them or control them, or without using them to draw attention to the helper through parallels in his own life. To 'soak up' sounds merely passive; but really to listen and go on listening as such anguish gushes out is very exhausting; yet, in the end, it offers the best chance of healing. Often we may be tempted, and from the best of motives, to get religion to do what we can't do ourselves. But we need to recognize the ambiguity of religion at this point. Gerald Priestland said that for him religion only increased his sense of worthlessness and guilt; that illness deepened the chasm between himself and God; and that a sick mind could only conceive a sickened religion. 'I am very much afraid', he said, 'there is little point in looking to faith and prayer for relief. In all my contacts, I have heard from only two people who claimed to have been helped by their faith. In my experience, Christianity is of no help: indeed, many find it to be an aggravation of their despair.' (In the end, however, it was 'the notion of Christ – even the Father – suffering with us, descending into the darkness, and very positively rising again' which helped to bring him through.)[1] In my experience, too, it isn't only that faith may be of little help to the depressive, and might even seem to make the sickness worse; it is also that a strong faith on the part of the helper might seem like a reproach, and increase guilt further. Consequently, any expression of the carer's faith may simply have to be in the way in which it informs and sustains the attitude of the carer. Again, the word 'sustains' is a key word, since perseverance to the end, the ability to go on giving of time and patience or, in a word, loving without counting the cost, is never more essential than in the case of the depressive. To withhold verbal expression of faith is very difficult for those to whom such expression comes naturally – but to withhold it out of love and care for the other person is a sign of greater faith still.

An important distinction is worth recognizing when we're tempted to 'use' religion as a means of therapy in cases like depression. It is valid in every sphere of religion and life, but particularly important when we're tempted to see religion as 'cure'. The researches of the psychologist Gordon Allport led him to ask the question why it was that 'on the average, churchgoers are more bigoted towards minority groups than non-churchgoers', whilst some are leaders in the fight against ethnic prejudice. (The obvious example of Desmond Tutu comes to mind.) Allport concluded that there are two basic types of religious orientation: one he calls extrinsic, the other intrinsic. Extrinsic religion is commitment to a faith that will serve your interests: it is something to use (for ceremony, family convenience or personal comfort), but not to live. 'It may be used to improve one's status, to bolster one's self-confidence'; in short, it is 'a shield for self-centredness'. Intrinsic religion, on the other hand, 'is not instrumental. It is not a means of handling fear, a mode of sociability and conformity, a sublimation of sex or a wish fulfilment. All these motives are somehow subordinated to an over-arching motive.' And that over-arching motive is the commitment of the whole person to the service of faith. 'Such religion does not exist to serve the person; rather the person is committed to serve it.'[2] It does not need much imagination to see that it is only the latter, intrinsic faith, which provides some still centre of support in life's most anxious moments.

Those anxious moments often provide the test of the depth and sort of a person's religious faith. It isn't only when we use religion as a cure that the extrinsic aspect shows itself, but whenever we make religion serve our purposes, for instance, when we see it chiefly as giving us hope, courage, resources to cope and so on. All these are by-products of a commitment, and the commitment is for its own sake.

So what is it that we as carers are offering to the depressive in our persevering work of absorbing his depression? Our very perseverance should help him or her finally not to lose hope and sink further into a pit of despair. He or she may come to feel that at least there is one person to whom, whatever they are like, they count and to whom they can relate, and that may enable them to modify their attitude towards other people as well. Since it is now agreed by many therapists of different schools of thought that depression is often frozen anger which people turn back on themselves instead of expressing, we may be able to encourage them to release that anger for us to absorb. (How often Christians run away from anger, rather than to try to absorb it!) One thing is certain: we can't jolly depressives out of their depression, and must not try. They cannot respond to that sort of warmth, and the nicer and pleasanter we try to be, the more depressed and anxious we make them. They can't cope with a friendliness which sometimes seems overdone, and false heartiness can postpone their recovery. On the other hand, there are several practical things we can encourage, over appearance, about diet and in encouraging depressives to accomplish some small task which is within their range, and which will partially restore their self-esteem when they find that they can be effective to that small degree.

In the end, there is no substitute for that loving relationship which will assure them that come what may, they will never be deserted, that in all the surrounding darkness there is a warm hand and just a pinpoint of light. Sometimes that relationship will be expressed in shared silence: just being quiet with the depressed, since, like those who are bereaved, they may really be beyond the reach of words.

Suicide

The word suicide is likely to raise a flutter of panic in many of us. That makes doubly important cool consideration of the question, as a preparation for any experience we may have. There is one important and neglected factor we especially need calmly to explore. Psychology and Christian faith, as we have seen, come together in agreeing that life is about the growth of human beings to maturity, and that that maturity consists of the business of making choices and accepting responsibility for them. We become fully ourselves through our moral choices. But if the real choice is the essence both of morality and maturity, then why not choice here, over the question of whether to die or not as well as in the myriad choices in life?

It isn't only our instinctive obligation to preserve life at all costs or the Christian insistence on the sanctity of life (even though the New Testament is very silent in condemnation of suicide) which prevents us from following the full implications of choice in human life to its logical conclusion. It is that, excepting some martyrs and Captain Oates going out into the blizzard, we find it difficult to think of a death that has been chosen as being in any sense honourable, as being the considered outcome of a total reflection on circumstances and issues. Yet we can all think of situations, certain illnesses, physical handicaps or emotional upheavals where we might wish to choose to die, where we might conclude that it would be better for the people and cases and institutions we hold dear if we were not around any more. And if we think of our lives as being in some way analogous to works of art, not to be spoilt by the introduction of material which is alien to the picture, and which cannot be integrated with the whole, then, bizarre though it sounds, suicide may complete the picture. I think that I have known two people whose suicides were the fruit of an agonizing reflection on what was in the best interests of all concerned and, not least, of the completeness of their own lives. And I believe that a society which is on the road to maturity will increasingly recognize and salute the responsibility of choice.

Now, of course, if that were all to be said, I could rightly be accused of talking simply (if not naively) on the lofty plane of ethical idealism, a Utopia of the distant future, rather than the messy relativities in which we are always immersed. But I've tried to isolate this matter of choice in order to try and lay bare the central issue, which so often gets hidden, and the implications of which we do not yet know how to handle. The truth is that, as with every other moral and ethical question, we can't turn up the easy answer in the back of the book, even the books of scripture. Suicide is a term that covers many different acts, widely varying in their moral quality. I have heard psychiatrists advance the dogma, without argument, that all suicides or suicide attempts are the result of pathological illness, which is a very convenient dogma since it neatly disposes of all moral questions which might be involved. Most of us will not be so easily satisfied, and will need to go on wrestling with the messy relativities. Clearly, some suicides seem to be the result of psychological compulsion, and can therefore be subject to moral judgment; some are actions which could technically be termed suicide, but which, if we were sufficiently courageous, we would see as being worthy of moral approval; some would seem simply to be cowardly and selfish; some we shall never understand.

For us as pastoral carers there may be two questions we need to keep in mind and – if we are granted the suitable opportunity – to pose. The first is to be as certain as possible that the depressed person is not simply acting under the impulse of a mood, and has seriously been helped to consider possibilities for the future; the second is whether the effect of their suicide on others for whom they most care has been carefully weighed. Choice is crucial; but we never exercise choice in a vacuum, and choice must always be made in the context of the welfare of others as well as ourselves – and perhaps, too, of the loss of any general or particular contribution we might make to the welfare of society as a whole. The guilt heaped on those closest to the person who commits suicide is often enormous ('there must have been something we could have done . . .'), and in many cases, it is guilt no more deserved by them than it is by the rest of us bound together in a network of human relationships which is often indifferent and uncaring.

I think there are twin dangers for us as we seek to care when there is a possibility of suicide: that of not taking it seriously enough and that of taking it too seriously. In the first case, our coolness may push the other person closer to the brink because it may be perceived not as coolness but as that emotional indifference of other people which caused the misery in the first place. In the second case, our judgment will be clouded by our sense of panic, and the clear-headedness which would be one of our chief assets will depart. So we will not try to cajole depressed persons out of suicide or use every artifice to distract them in some activity outside themselves. Nor will we, and this is a great temptation to good Christians, use Christian arguments to try to dissuade them, or worse still, threaten them with the consequences of eternal punishment. We shall keep as closely and fully as possible to the two questions. Sometimes we may find it helpful to be allowed to admit that we have at some time or another considered suicide; without triggering off condemnation or panic in the listener, this can be very significant in breaking the ice-cool ring which shuts them off from relationship. And we shall also recognize that on several occasions we shall be in touch with people whose talk of suicide is a bid for relationship, a cry for help. It isn't safe, as statistics show, to assume that it's only those who don't talk about it who commit suicide, but we shall almost certainly be involved with those who over-dramatize their situation in their desperate search for solace.

I recognize that the practical problems with which suicide leaves us are immense, and that even to write about them at all is somehow to trivialize them. But as pastoral carers, we can help the slow process of making more opportunities for freer choice without the crippling effects of guilt and failure in us all. My own experience tells me that suicide is more connected with a loss of a sense of self-worth than it is with anything we do; and (I necessarily repeat myself) that sense of self-worth is only indirectly attained by the way other people value us. I find it hard to take that a society which allows for so much devaluation of persons, and consequently pushes some in the direction of self-destruction, should at the same time multiply the guilt with which other people have to live, once that act of suicide has taken place.

10

Pastoral Care in Illness

If the titles of this and the next chapters look all too predictable in a book on pastoral care, let me excuse myself on the grounds that I am looking at the scene not so much with a carer's eye as with the eye of the cared for, the patient, chiefly from my own experience. That experience has taught me to be more reticent in my conclusions than is generally allowed for, especially in books on Christian healing, and makes me want to avoid that familiar and overworked phrase 'the sick and the suffering' which suggests that unrealistic distinction between us (the healthy) and the rest . . .

The quality of our lives, our 'health', cannot simply refer to the absence in them of physical disabilty. Most of us know people who do not appear to have anything wrong with them physically, but we still feel that things are not 'right' with them. It may seem to be the wrong set of values which animates them; emotional blockages which inhibit them; nervous fears and anxieties which paralyse them. And if we were pressed, we should have a natural hesitation about applying to them the term 'healthy'. On the other hand, I have a vivid mental picture of an invalid, paralysed from birth, who spent all her days lying on a trolley-stretcher, completely dependent on others for all her needs. She was a frail and twisted midget of a lady but she was visited by many people, and especially young people. It was not that they came to offer her consolation and cheer her up: it was that she gave of herself to them in wisdom and love. It was as if they recognized in her, without being able to articulate it, health and wholeness which showed through her physical weakness. We can never shut up the concept of health in mere satisfactory physical functioning.

The dramatic cures effected by some 'spiritual healers' can lead to over-enthusiasm for that one form of healing. It can undervalue the way in which God's spirit can work through orthodox medicine and of the way in which the humdrum work of GPs brings great relief and comfort to large numbers of people. Further, the dangers of the miraculous cure is that we can come to see the power of God as primarily (or worse still exclusively) present there, whereas it is equally important to see the power of God continually sustaining those who suffer and who in this life may never be cured. There is an even worse scenario: when, as sometimes happens, enthusiasts for certain forms of healing suggest that some hidden sin or guilt must inevitably be the cause of the illness.

There is another difficulty. Any attempt to portray pastoral care in this area can lead to a major misunderstanding. It can indirectly suggest that all that is necessary is that we do certain things aright, put certain rules into practice, as it were. I remember coming across a book containing a list of no less than fifty do's and don'ts which we all need to observe in visiting those who are ill – including some warnings about knocking before entering the room and not chewing gum! The trouble is that even when we observe all the rules (and many of them are just plain commonsense) we may still be of little help to the patient. For, as in all pastoral care and counselling, it is the quality of the meeting between two people which counts for more than anything else: what we are able to give of ourselves to the other and in giving, to receive.

It came as an exciting discovery to me when I learnt that the same Greek word is used in the New Testament to denote three states which we sometimes treat independently. To be saved, to be healed, and to be made whole, are all described by that one word. But the word used for 'cure' is quite different. The word 'cure' merely suggests getting better from some physical ailment, restoring some part of our body to its proper functioning. But being healed, saved, made whole, this is an added and positive dimension. When Jesus cured the ten lepers and only one returned to give thanks, the implication was that that one man was made whole. Why? Because he had been able to express an insight, a dimension of gratitude, wonder and humility to which the others were blind and which is an essential part of being made whole 'Were there not ten cleansed?',

'Thy faith hath made thee whole.'¹ In my experience, as a coronary bypass patient, I found the process of healing to be directly analogous to the process of conversion, or being saved. A process, that is, which results in a different orientation in life, a complete reversal to the direction in which you are travelling. The onset of illness generates self-absorption: my horizon becomes bounded by my aches and pains, my anxiety about the outcome of the illness. Paradoxically, other people's concern, which is wonderfully supportive and which should take me out of myself, increases my self-concern. They continually ask me how I am, and as I repeatedly tell my story, I tend not only to exaggerate, but to get things out of proportion. My self-obsession grows. And to be centred on self is to be un-saved.

When the crisis is passed and the operation safely over, the long slow journey to recovery starts. It is a process of gradually turning outwards to face the world once more, the shedding of that obsessive self-concern. The progress is not even. Self-concern, which sometimes takes the form of self-pity, still pulls me back. I am loathe to come out of my cocoon and to surrender my cosy dependence. I still want to cling to that weakness and illness which has created an identity for me, won me other peoples' concern and sympathy and given me significance.

Jesus asked the man who had been crippled for thirty-eight years and who was lying beside the pool of Bethesda, 'Do you *want* to recover?'² We usually assume that people naturally want to recover, but experience shows that there are some who, at the same time that they complain about their sickness, also, perhaps secretly, fear recovery. It will mean surrending their protection and dependency. Perverse as it may seem to say so, some forms of illness can have considerable attractions. A friend of mine used to have a recurring dream whenever he felt unhappy. He would dream that he was a cripple in a wheelchair, and this always presented itself not as a fearful possibility but as an attractive one, since as an invalid, people would take care of him and not expect too much of him.

In the end, recovery happens, through a grace offered to me in the continuing love of other people and of the God who inspires both them and me. My healing and my conversion are one. Of course, I am never completely 'healed', any more than I experience a finished work of salvation. 'Are you *being* saved?' has always seemed to me to be a more legitimate question to ask than 'Are you *saved*?' – if we feel we have to ask the question at all!

Further, we are not talking simply about a private religious experience or seeing salvation simply in narrow religious terms. Once we take the New Testament relationship between being 'healed', 'saved' and 'made whole' seriously, we see that they all refer to all that we are in our relationships, as we grow into the love of God which is embodied in Jesus Christ. The healing process is continuous, unfinished to the grave, and will never be completed until the whole of creation is transformed. The New Testament sees beyond the healing of individuals to the restoration of God's creation in Jesus. So, 'salvation in the sense of personal and social "wholeness" is synonymous with the coming of the kingdom of God'.[3] I cannot claim to be healed whilst the rest of creation 'groans and travails',[4] for I am part of that creation and bear a measure of responsibility for it. In any case, if I am to live with some physical infirmity, given the grace of the cure, that is an inspiration and call to service, not simply the occasion for private relief and thanksgiving. I realize myself as part of that 'body of men and women enlisted to fight under His banner against sin, the world and the devil, cleansed of their own sins in order that they may be able to forget themselves in sharing in His interests in the rescuing and perfecting of His creation'.[5] Notice that when Jesus cured someone that was not the end of the matter. It was as if he always had his eye on the person's future. 'Thy faith hath made thee whole,' his most characteristic saying after he had performed such a miracle, was some indication of the life they were now to lead. Blind Bartimeus, we are told, 'followed him in the way'[6] – and 'the way' was the earliest description of Christian faith and life. Paul Tillich speaks of those who made their 'self-surrender to the healing power in Jesus':

He did not keep them, as a good helper should never do. He gave them back to themselves, as new creatures, healed and whole. And when he died, He left a group of people who, in spite of much anxiety and discord and weakness and guilt, had the certitude that they were healed, and that the healing power among them was great enough to conquer individuals and nations all over the world. We belong to these people, if we are grasped by the new reality which has appeared in him. We have his healing powers ourselves.[7]

We are healed – to serve.

The turning outwards, away from self, to God and to concern for others, is both salvation and healing. It is also wholeness. The disjointedness, the alienation, the being at odds with other people and oneself is the very opposite of health: 'I've fallen apart,' 'I'm only half the person I was,' 'I'm all shot to bits,' we say in times of stress. That which draws me together and unifies me is the magnetic centre of the love of God. As I am drawn to him, I am drawn together as a person made whole, however imperfectly expressed. But again, I am not to glory in my increasing wholeness. The more I respond to God's love in Christ, the more whole I become, the more sensitive I become, too, and paradoxically, the more I shall suffer. Any increase in my sensitivity to love also increases my capacity for being hurt. Healing, salvation, wholeness: all for the glory of God, the welfare of others and often for the increase of my own suffering.

We need always to be as deep and all-embracing as this in our own pastoral care of those who are ill. The twentieth-century philosophy which affects us all tends to look on pain and suffering as unqualified evil, and holds out to us the hope of a pleasurable, pain-free existence as the highest hope we can entertain. But without surrendering to any masochistic strains still lurking in the deep recesses of Christian faith, there is a higher good than such a philosophy of pleasure allows: that we shall all attain to that maturity, humanity, wholeness which is our individual and unique destiny – or (reluctant as I am to use the phrase, since it has been used to justify so much evil in his name) God's will for us. Again, we distinguish between God's will to cure and God's will to heal. In order to realize that destiny and to be in conformity with God's will, it may be that we shall not be cured. Two illustrations from the New Testament have helped me. The first is the way in which in St John's Gospel, Jesus says to the disciples about the blind man, 'He was born blind that

God's power might be displayed in curing him':[8] and the second the way in which St Paul says that he has prayed three times that what he describes as 'a sharp pain in my body' should be removed, and the answer he has received is that God's grace is all he needed.[9] In his case God's power was not displayed in curing him – but 'in weakness'. The implication is that the blind man came alive to God through Jesus' miraculous intervention, whereas for St Paul, in order, as he says, 'to save him from being unduly elated' by the mystical revelations he has enjoyed, he was being helped to grow through the pain and the suffering which would not be taken away.

So when a cure does not happen, instead of interpreting it either as a sign that God does not answer our prayer, or of our own lack of faith, we may be able to come through it to see that something is being wrought which is to our eternal glory. There are graces of patience and perseverance to be grown into, a courage to be won, and a humility and interdependence to be learnt, through that circumscribed and limited life which will inevitably be ours. That acceptance should drive out any self-pity, for it will be looking for the positive in the disability and finding unexpected sources of blessing.

So with this background, how do we visit those who are ill? It can hardly be said to be everybody's natural vocation although we all do it at some time or another. But more people would, I believe, be ready to take on a commitment to visit a few sick people regularly, if they were given proper encouragement and help. We are not very good at that sort of informal education for lay pastoral care, for we tend to think that it can all be done by the light of nature (or Holy Spirit) –and that to offer help is somehow to diminish spontaneity. The contrary is true in my experience. True spontaneity is increased because confidence is heightened. So what guidelines can we offer? I have already used the term 'sensitive visiting' and I can find no better. Sensitivity depends on so many things. It depends, first, on the unselfconscious realization of the presence of God in the meeting with the sick person. It is not that we 'take God with us'; he is there already, always 'going before us'; it is for us to rest in the knowledge that he is there and so have confidence to be ourselves. Second, sensitivity depends on certain very practical things: a willingness, above all, to see and to listen to what is going on inside the patient, paying close attention to the time we spend with him or her, that it is neither too short, as if we wish to escape as quickly as possible, having 'done our duty' and are now able to make a 'job done' tick on our list, nor too long, which is an equal danger. I have discovered how tiring company can be in convalescence and sometimes all the good which is achieved by the visit is wrecked by the fatigue engendered by a visit which is too long. Again, without in any sense becoming unnatural, sick visiting is not the place for general conversation about everything and anything under the sun. Jo Ann Kelly Smith, a cancer sufferer, put the matter like this:

> When anyone comes to visit me, I don't want him to come with his own agenda ... I often get the feeling that before people enter my room, they try to decide what to say. I don't want to hear their concerns. I want them to empty their heads of their own ideas. When you visit a sick person, fill your head with thoughts about that person, your care for him and what you can do to get in touch with him ... If you just go in and listen, they'll do all the 'saying', because they really want to talk about themselves. They need to get in touch with their feelings and they need to tell it to another human being.[10]

Of course, it is right for visitors to try to open windows on the world through their conversation, especially if the patients are long-stay patients, but generally, visiting is the opportunity for focussing on the patient, gently eliciting what they are feeling so that they know you are truly with them, able to feel on your pulse, as it were, what it is like to be them at that moment. Most of us are guilty of what I call 'distance visiting', which is little more than conventional chatter and cheeriness, unconsciously designed to protect us from real exposure to the other person. Only empathy sustains. Those visitors are most helpful who say little but are 'at one with you', are imaginative about your practical needs, who bear with them a confidence in a God of love who never abandons you whatever the pain, and who give you the confidence that they will still be with you even when they are physically absent. Sometimes they will pray with you, using a simple form and few words commending you to God's love. Sometimes such prayer would seem forced and unnatural, more aimed at formally 'getting things right' than being sensitive to the moment. Sensitivity, of course, is not a guide to certainty and there is no guarantee that we shall always make the right decision. But it is always a better guide where persons are concerned than any rule of thumb, even if you pay the price, as I have often done, and realize in retrospect the mistakes I have made. The motive for sick visiting is not a 'churchy' motive at all. In humility and grace, it is to be one demonstration (amongst others, it is to be hoped, but sometimes *the* demonstration) of God's love and concern for that person, through the visitor's genuine love and concern. If we visit 'to witness' or implicitly 'to interest the patient in the church', then in however subtle a form we are using manipulation and the patient is being treated as an object and not a subject which is always inexcusable in Christian terms. If the motivation for visiting is not right, then nothing will be right and the patient will see the exercise as the pious charade it really is. On the other hand, to give time, patience, and indeed, of oneself to another simply out of love, to respond to God's love: that will be seen for the grace and graciousness it implies. Nothing influences a person for good more than such an act of grace which is, by its very nature, undeserved and unsought.

One of the gifts which the Holy Spirit, the Comforter, surely bestows on us as Christians is that of being able to sustain, and this is especially important during the period of convalescence. At the point of crisis, during the first onset of illness, or prior to and immediately after an operation, the patient is very often surrounded, if not overwhelmed, by loving concern. Once the crisis is past the flood of concern appears to become a trickle, if it does not dry up altogether. (This is not to say that the concern is not there: it just does not continue to be demonstrated.) But the healing process is slow and protracted, however well things seem to be going for the patient. Its very slowness implies a sustaining process which is persevering, and just when the patient is feeling most frustrated, appearing to be making such little and slow progress, then the supportive resources may fail him or her most. Convalescence is the period when it is possible to draw lessons from the experience of illness and advance in self-knowledge, and so put the illness into perspective. But if this is to happen then the patient needs to be able to explore these things with the help of someone who is prepared to work through them with him or her in conversation. It is just this sort of resource our visiting could supply. Again, there is some analogy with the conversion process. The long, slow process of growth after conversion is not given anything like the emphasis it deserves; by comparison with the dramatic crisis of conversion, it is dull and unexciting, but fundamental to the Christian life.

It seems to me that Charles Causley's sixth visitor in his poem 'Ten Types of Hospital Visitor' beautifully captures the spirit of our visiting.

The sixth visitor says little,
Breathes reassurance,
Smiles securely,
Carries no black passport of grapes
Or visa of chocolate. Has a clutch
Of clean washing.
Unobtrusively stows it
In the locker; searches out more.
Talks quietly to the sister
Out of sight, out of earshot, of the patient.
Arrives punctually as a tide
Does not stay the whole hour.

Even when she has gone
The patient seems to sense her there: an upholding
    Presence.[11]

That surely says it all: 'an upholding Presence'. A presence nourished by the Presence of the One from whose love, however dark and threatening life may seem, we can never be separated. And that presence goes with intense practicality which does not need words or conventional gifts to give confidence either to the helper or to the patient.

I can testify to the truth of Charles Causley's description. Having had five or six spells in hospital during the past few years, I feel confident I could write a long article 'On Being Visited by Clergymen and Ministers'! And on looking back on two spells in a men's hospital ward, I contrast two visits, one from an agnostic and one from a clergyman. The agnostic hates hospitals and finds the sight of blood or the story of operations too painful to bear. He only stayed five minutes but I knew what it had cost him emotionally to come at all and he did what was the most helpful thing anyone could have done then – left me with some five and ten penny coins for the travelling phone and for the newsboy. He had used his imagination and sensitivity to my real needs. I contrast that experience with a visit I endured from an earnest clergyman who made it plain that he thought he was doing his duty, wearied me with a long account of what he had been up to in the church conference the previous week, prayed with me in formal fashion, and had an afterthought after he had said goodbye and had started to walk down the ward: 'Is there anything you want?'

As with visit, so with prayer. Prayer for those who are ill is a partnership in which being prayerful and being practical go hand in hand. But there is always an inbuilt theological dilemma in praying for other people. Here we must go back to St Augustine's maxim, 'Without God, we cannot. Without us, God will not.' 'Intercession is a prayer in which the person who prays both asks God to act on behalf of the person or cause for whom he intercedes and also makes himself available as secondary cause through whom God could act in answering the prayer.'[12] God and the person who prays are, in other words, partners in the enterprise.

And we should pray simply. Intercession is holding a person in the presence of God's love, being with him together in that presence. Nothing else is necessary. Simple, and extremely powerful: to be surrounded by God's love, consciously to be upheld and supported by praying people makes an incalculable difference, especially when facing a major operation. I find now that for people who are ill, I can no longer pray that something will happen to him or her. The only relevant prayer would be that he or she be made whole, but as we know that this is the will of God in any case, the phrase is superfluous. How long has prayer suffered from a superfluity of words! Jesus himself warned us against our 'much speaking'. In praying for those who are ill, it is surely sufficient to name those individuals followed by periods of silence. Where prayer groups exist, it is easier for them to do this in their meetings than in the course of public worship and many prayer groups do this very well. When they specifically meet to 'pray for the sick' there is always the danger, of course, that they focus exclusively on 'sickness' and become morbidly centred on it. I have noticed that good and well-intentioned individuals can come to love passing on 'bad news' about other peoples' illnesses – and this danger exists, multiplied, in a group unless great care is taken to focus positively on God, his love and his wish to heal. There is another and subtler danger still in intercession and intercessory groups, a danger to which Monica Furlong points: that of

> . . . taking an inflated view of ourselves. It is a short step from praying for other people in their troubles to feeling that one has some sort of control over their troubles, and a short step from controlling their troubles to having some control, however benevolent, over them. Or we may have a different temptation to somehow claim them as ours – our protégés, our lame dogs, our cures. No sort of intercession which does not leave the other person in a state of total freedom is any good.[13]

Finally, reflecting on my own recent experience as a patient, it is the vulnerability, the fragility of life and the weakness of which I have been most conscious. It has been a vulnerability hard to bear, but my pastoral experience should have taught me better. I can see more clearly now how my pastoral caring, and all 'helping' ministries, can push us towards an invulnerability which will both protect us and feed our sense of self-importance. My illness has shown up that pretension to invulnerability for what it is worth – or rather, for what it is not worth. For all of us, the wounds of illness can be a well from which we can draw deep resources of compassion and empathy. It is those wounds which will help us to be readily available as instruments of healing, however inadequate, in the lives of other people.

11

Pastoral Care of the Terminally Ill

Again, in exploring the care of the terminally ill, I want to approach it from the point of view of the patient's experience. Here, I count myself fortunate that from an early age I have been made aware of the frontier of death. My father died of a coronary thrombosis when I was six, and my relatives' attempts to conceal or soften the reality of what had happened ('Daddy's up there, watching everything that you do . . .' was the only explanation I was given) only heightened my childish impression of the strangeness of death. It was an impression which haunted me for some time afterwards, and looking back on the experience from this distance, I find the silence which surrounded the event disturbing. It was a classic instance of evasion, done for the best of motives, a sort of blind unwillingness to weave the experience of death into any coherent pattern of living. I was forced to keep my elementary questionings to myself and in later life this experience has enabled me to see the psychological harm we inflict upon ourselves and others by our denial of death, or our refusal to face its reality.

That reality I was forced to face shortly after my twenty-first birthday, when the RAF twin-engined Beaufighter in which I was a navigator was shot down by anti-aircraft fire whilst we were strafing a ship in a Greek harbour. Our port engine had been set on fire, and as the pilot put the aircraft down on the water (I remember seeing the tail-plane come apart from the rest of the aircraft) I sank inside it. I can vividly call to mind the way in which I 'waited for the end', reflecting that it had not really been such a bad twenty-one years. Then, almost instantaneously, the struggle to survive got the better of me, although to this day I have no idea out of which part of the aircraft I emerged to join my pilot who, badly burnt in the face and arms, was already swimming in the salt water. Rescued by speed-boats with machine-guns pointing at us (whilst we swam in the opposite direction: hope springs eternal . . .) and seeing another of our aircraft on the raid burning ashore, with two dead occupants, a new chapter of our careers started in a German military hospital, and finished in a German POW camp.

My memory of the whole incident, of that experience of momentarily coming so close to death through drowning, is crystal clear: incredible as it sounds, for I am the least courageous of men, there was, alongside the sense of panic, a sense of completion and of fulfilment. And that at twenty-one years of age! It was as if I saw my life from an 'end perspective' – and, contrary to all natural expectations and certainly, to rationality, it added up, made sense.

Then, fourteen years ago, after a night of increasing pain, I was taken into a hospital intensive care unit with a heart attack. Again, I had a surprising sense of contentment, as if this might well be the end of the first part of a long journey. It was not in any sense, I think, a complacent feeling that I had passed the 'examination of life' with credit, if not with distinction. Paradoxically, it was my realization of unfulfilled possibilities, of the continual process of learning and unlearning that my life had involved, of the tantalizingly few glimpses of communion with God I felt I had enjoyed, which made me feel both satisfied about this first part, and also gave me some hope and assurance that the good work which had only just been started in my transformation into the image of God would be continued beyond this life.

Far from being oppressed by this, then, I count myself fortunate that my experiences have kept me constantly aware of the frontier of death, quite apart from my own pastoral involvement in other people's bereavements. That does not make life dark and depressing as it sounds, but quite the contrary. It is our recognition of that frontier which helps us to see a deeper meaning in life, to refuse to take it for granted, or to trivialize it. A richer quality of life emerges as it is looked at from the perspective of death. To have a proper valuing of life is surely part of what it means to be healed: for it means that we are not 'blocking off' or refusing to look at that which we fear or find too terrible to contemplate. Healed persons are those who, however hard and painful the circumstances, never ultimately let go of the confidence that whatever the emergency they face, even the 'ultimate' emergency of death, they are not separated from the love of God. They are, in other words, those who have integrated the certainty of death into the living of their lives. Lily Pincus, when eighty-three years old, wrote: 'If I think about death, it is with the hope that I will still be truly alive when it comes. To be aware of death makes life more precious and asking questions about the meaning of life more urgent.'[1] Dr Glin Bennett, at a lesser age, shares that view:

> Those who have in any way come close to death thereafter speak in a special way about life, and manage to live fully in the Eternal Everchanging Present, taking each day as it comes. I would find it hard to savour the richness of summer without reference to the winter that preceded it and which will follow it. Day would be hard to imagine without night. As I become more aware of death because I am getting older and encounter more people who are dying, so life becomes richer. This is not because each day I move nearer to the end of my life but rather because the reality of death intensifies the reality of living.[2]

In the last television interview he gave in early Spring 1994, shortly before he died, Dennis Potter poignantly expressed the 'nowness' of everything, looked at from the perspective of death.

> Below my window in Ross, when I'm working in Ross, for example, there at this season, the blossom is out in full now . . . it's a plum tree, it looks like apple blossom but it's white, and looking at it, instead of saying 'oh that's nice blossom' . . . last week looking at it through the window when I'm writing, I *see* it is the whitest, frothiest, blossomest blossom that there ever could be, and I can see it. Things are both more trivial than they ever were, and more important than they ever were, and the difference between the trivial and the important doesn't seem to matter. But the nowness of everything is absolutely wondrous, and if people could *see* that, you know. There's no way of telling you, you have to

experience it, but the glory of it, if you like, the comfort of it, the reassurance . . .³

So, in view of this recognition of the 'blessed boundary of death', it isn't difficult to ask what needs we would have if we were terminal care patients, in order better to respond as carers to those needs. There would, I think, be four particular needs.

First, I would need gently to be helped to know the truth of my condition. I stress the word 'gently' since most of us know situations where, in order to get an unpleasant task over quickly, patients have been told the stark truth, and then left unsupported. Most of us would wish to strive for a situation in which patient and relatives are aware, rather than living in a dishonest 'conspiracy of silence' (perhaps deception would be a better word), so that fears can properly be expressed on both sides and real communication is possible. Few situations are more ludicrous than those in the middle of which I have sometimes found myself, when the relatives aren't telling the patient because he couldn't stand it, and the patient isn't letting on to the relatives because 'they'd be upset!' But it can't simply be right to insist always on telling all, willy-nilly. A person's approach is unique to that person. And the actual and full circumstances of a person's attitude to life must be taken into consideration. If, for example, a person has previously not been able to look death in the face, and studiously avoided it, then the difficulty of helping him to come to terms with it is immeasurably increased. And any violent tearing away of the patient's defence can't possibly be right; indeed, it may even be right (at least temporarily) to support the defence mechanism, since it is the one real resource the patient has for coping, and if that goes, there is nothing on which to fall back. That is a sure recipe for final hopelessness and despair. Of course, there must always be kept open the possibility of change; and for some, death really can be the final stage of growth, as we've seen. But very often in our pastoral care we shall be supporting weakness which started in problems stretching back a long way into the patient's earlier life – problems which might have been resolved then, but which have hardened into a permanent attitude to life. It is too late to begin to resolve those problems and modify attitudes in terminal care. My conviction is that it is *how* people are told any truth about their condition which matters most. Nurses working in terminal care often have the experience of being asked the question 'Am I going to die?' at the most inconvenient of moments, often, for instance, when their physical and emotional resources are at a low ebb, perhaps at two o'clock in the morning. The guideline is telling as much truth as it is thought the patient can bear with gentleness and care.

Secondly, I would need to know that I am not going to be abandoned on the lonely road to death, that I am not going simply to be left as a hopeless case, for whom nothing more can be done. I have had patients complain to me, half jokingly, about their relatives, who, they say, 'look on me as if I were already dead'. Here the Hospice Movement's insistence that we live until the moment we die is crucial. To me an unforgettable scene was that of hearing how a lady had had her hair permed the day before she died, and I well remember the mother of one of our choirboys, who was dying of cancer, but who was always determined to have her make-up as perfect as possible right up to the day she died.

It isn't perhaps so much fear of being physically abandoned: much more of being emotionally abandoned because of this feeling that there is nothing more than can be done. 'Being there', a fundamental in all our caring for the ill and the dying, implies that we won't seek to avoid close contact with the dying person. In this context, touch is obviously vital. (Touch is, in fact, the oldest skill of the doctor, now of course largely forgotten in the days of technological medicine.) And 'proper' touch, proper because it is easy to touch in a patronizing spirit, as a natural, unconditional gesture, can create a sense of personal value, of worth – even in the most extreme cases – as nothing else can. There are times when touch alone seems able to communicate with the patient, and it is our touch which will assure them that they have not been abandoned.

I would need, thirdly, to find someone to listen. Knowing that my death is near makes me realize some of the many ways in which I have failed other people, my unresolved conflicts, and the many loose ends in my life. So it may be that I need, before the curtain falls, to get something off my chest which has been troubling me for years

– and which I have never dealt with properly. But the classic response when patients are on the point of unloading some difficult and perhaps embarrassing material is to cut it short: 'Don't bother with that now: it's all over and done with.' But it isn't, and it needs airing to someone who will listen and hear the patient out. Release from guilt can happen when the person is truly able to confide in another whose qualities of love and care and openness and receptivity inspire the giving of such confidence. I can well remember a situation in a particular hospice, in which a post-graduate student of mine, engaged in a PhD thesis, discovered that those who listened best were often the cleaners, who had a natural, first-name relationship with the patients and with whom, as with no other members of staff, they were able to talk freely about any subject. That hospice took the matter to heart, and from then on, engaged voluntary pastoral assistants who were there simply to develop sufficient confidence in the patients to allow them to talk freely.

My fourth need would be for someone to share my helplessness. The position is that everyone has done their best: but the doctors, the nurses, the relatives are powerless to alter my condition. I am going to die. And in that situation the person who is going to be able to help most is the person who will share my helplessness and not shrink from it. As I have mentioned before, there is a paradox here: it is sometimes when we are feeling most unhelpful, even helpless, that we are of most help.

From her great experience as a consultant in hospice work, Sheila Cassidy comes to this conclusion:

Much of the time I must work with my hands empty, drawing upon my own personal resources to comfort anguished patients. This means that I am often very informal with them. I have long since shed my professional facade because I now know that patients see right through such armour and what they really respect is that heady mixture, competence and compassion. Sometimes I think of myself like the wretched mother pelican, pulling the feathers out of my breast until the blood flows to feed my starving children. I believe that it is this drawing upon one's own resources that makes all the difference in the care of the terminally ill. The hospital specialist may legitimately say, 'I'm sorry, there is nothing more that I can do to help you.' Specialists in palliative care, however, must accept that the buck stops with them; they have made a covenant with their people to accompany them until they die. Like the Lord, whose hands they must be, they must say:

> . . . the mountains may depart,
> the hills be shaken,
> but my love for you will never leave you
> and my covenant of peace with you will never be shaken
> (Isa. 54.10).[4]

It might be helpful to identify the various stages which have been isolated in the dying process. But it is important not to take these stages dogmatically. There may be variations in the length of each stage, and there isn't necessarily gradual or uninterrupted progress from one to the other. Indeed, in some circumstances, the stages may be blurred.

Denial ('I'll be back at work before long') may be to protect the patient or his relatives from the impact of the shock: it is a defence mechanism which allows him still the possibility of hope, and the ability to begin to adjust to it.

Isolation ('You don't know what it's like: I have to go through it myself') is the intense loneliness which gradual recognition of the condition brings, which may be heightened if carers bring into it much of their own anxieties about death.

Anger is the next response: 'Why should it happen to me?' The angry mood reinforces any natural inclination we have to avoid the patient, because it is hard to endure, just at the point where he most needs befriending.

The *bargaining* phase is the point at which the patient seems to be beginning to come to terms with his own death, but on conditions. ('I wouldn't mind so much – if only . . .' It's the 'if only' which is the most common phrase.)

The bargaining phase can slip into *depression*. ('Nothing does any good'.) It is now that there is the greatest temptation to play the part of 'cheering up', again diverting his attention from his real and pressing situation to something else which we feel will comfort and placate him.

Acceptance ('You know I'm going, don't you?') is the final stage, in which the patient has begun to make his own preparation for death, when he seems ready to let go, the arrival of a stage which may be conveyed through a smile, or touch, when words may be difficult.

Going back to my earlier experience, I am sure that we should hesitate to be involved in care for the dying if we haven't come fully to terms with our own dying. Unless we can say, and mean it, not that '*we* are all going to die', but '*I* am going to die'; in other words, unless we have faced up to the 'blessed boundary of death', and are able to contemplate a world going on happily without us, we may bring our own conflicts into our caring, and this will prove a stumbling block to those whom we are most trying to help. Woody Allen expressed that sense of conflict best when he made his classic remark: 'I don't mind dying; I just don't want to be there when it happens.' Of course, there is rightly a mystery about death which we will never fathom, but if we can look at death with a steady eye, we can help people, again paradoxically, to come to a state of being healed in the act of dying.

Finally, there is an important consequence in all this for Christian faith, and the way it is taught in our churches. There must be a greater willingness to explore the subject of dying, and at greater depth, in preaching and teaching. My own research indicates that the subject is hardly ever explored. And when it is explored, I discovered that it was always treated simply as a prelude to the realization of the hope of eternal life, rather than having significance in itself for the living of life on this earth. Do I exaggerate if I say that there is a form of concentration on that hope which is little more than escapism? Increasing expectation of life in the twentieth century has delivered us from cruder expressions of that hope, and few of us would now want to go along with the old burial service phrase about delivering our brethren 'out of the miseries of this sinful world'. But there is a temptation, I find, to preach and teach about the Christian hope of eternal life in a way which subtly ignores the reality of death. I suggest that we need to speak more about the fear of dying, the process of dying, and the meaning of death. To come to terms with the certainty of death is to see realistically the rich possibilities in life itself. Then we can also see more clearly the hope of that eternal life of which here on earth we have a foretaste, and with which ordinary life is shot through and occasionally, transformed.

12

Pastoral Care of the Bereaved

Any adequate model of pastoral care, I have suggested, must depend on our empathy, our willingness to be vulnerable, to be self-disclosing, and to share in the helplessness of the other person.

We can test this, for instance, in a difficult situation with which we may have to deal: the pastoral care of those who have been suddenly bereaved through a coronary thrombosis or road accident. There has been established in recent years some general pattern of bereavement with certain, well-defined, stages. The first stage, obviously, is that of numbness and denial. The bereaved person cannot take in the fact of the death, and this seems to have little to do with whether the person has died suddenly or slowly. The period can last as long as a month but is usually about a week or ten days. In this state of shock when the numbness is heightened often by the generous use of tranquillisers, and when practical arrangements have to be made about the funeral and the immediate future, rational conversation may scarcely be possible. What is it then that we can offer? Obviously it will not be words (which will scarcely be able to communicate, in any case) or any short cuts to healing. Dietrich Bonhoeffer's distinction between the ultimate and penultimate word is most relevant here:

> When I am with someone who has suffered a bereavement, I often decide to adopt a 'penultimate' attitude, particularly when I am dealing with Christians, remaining silent as a sign that I share in the bereaved man's helplessness in the face of such a grievous event, and not speaking the biblical words of comfort which are, in fact, known to me and available to me. Why am I often unable to open my mouth, when I ought to give expression to the ultimate?

And why, instead, do I decide on an expression of thoroughly penultimate human solidarity? Is it from mistrust of the power of the ultimate word? Is it from fear of men? Or is there some good, positive reason for such an attitude, namely, that my knowledge of the word, my having it at my fingertips, in other words my being, so to speak, spiritually master of the situation, bears only the appearance of the ultimate, but is in reality itself something entirely penultimate? Does one not in some cases, by remaining deliberately in the penultimate, perhaps point all the more generally to the ultimate, which God will speak in His own time (though indeed even then through a human mouth)?[1]

What we have to offer, again, is our presence. The bereaved will take from us, from the depths of what they have known of us or see in us, something of what they need at that particular time. It is not so much formal religion even the committed are looking for then. It is the assurance that still, in the midst of their grievous loss, all is well and this is communicated by presence, by our sense of inner peace but not complacency, by our looks, by our touch. A young doctor told me recently that when the daughter of one of her patients died at only a week old, all she could do was to sit on the floor with the mother for an hour as they wept together. Unorthodox medicine; excellent therapy. Presence releases as well as comforts and it will communicate our willingness to receive whatever the bereaved feels like expressing at that moment. (Incidentally, how much are we conditioned to bottle things up and keep things under, for the sake of other people? It is an odd irony that the one who is suffering most often thinks more of the 'helpers' and so restrains the tears.)

Perhaps *absorb* is the one word which catches the attitude I seek to describe. I use the word advisedly as being one of our greatest pastoral gifts, time-consuming and emotionally draining though it be. To be able to absorb other peoples' feelings without reflecting them is a great resource. In Susan Hill's moving novel of a young widow, Ruth, and her first year of sudden bereavement, *In the Springtime of the Year*,[2] it is her younger brother-in-law, Joe, who does quietly the practical jobs that need to be done – making the tea, lighting the fire, collecting the eggs – but who says least and absorbs most Ruth's moods of anger, guilt and frustration. We need to be able to absorb other peoples' depressions and today, especially, we may have to absorb a lot from people who feel that they have been hurt or abandoned by the church. Such absorption is at the heart of forgiveness. Jesus on the cross absorbed all the feelings of hatred which were loosed upon him, and his response 'Father, forgive them for they do not know what they are doing'[3] stopped the power of evil to produce more evil. But continuing to absorb someone's pain and anger can be exhausting and the costliness of the situation may want to make us cut the business short, using old clichés, dragging in religious concepts to relieve us rather than help the bereaved. Above all, our pastoral care of the suddenly bereaved implies that we ourselves have come to terms as fully as possible with our own dying and death. That will be our support when we are alongside the bereaved, with them in their weakness and in ours.

Life is a succession of small bereavements: we are losing all the time. So, unlike the process of dying, a process into which we have not yet entered, but simply done our best to come to terms with, the process of bereavement is something of which we all have experience. We have already mentioned the first stage of numbness and shock and the support appropriate to it. To complete the picture: the second stage is the stage where there may be intense feelings of yearning for the dead person; feelings of anger with the doctors, the hospital and the relatives – and even paradoxically, with the deceased himself for having left the bereaved 'like this'. And feelings of guilt begin to emerge, as there is plenty of time to look back on what the bereaved did or failed to do. Post-bereavement guilt can become an intractable problem in that there is no one to whom one can make reparation, and outside a religious framework of confession and forgiveness there is no obvious mechanism with which to deal with the problem. We can assume too easily that the relationship has been happy and fulfilling – and this can produce paroxysms of guilt in good people, especially since they will be expected to grieve in a conventional manner. (It reminds me of Albert Camus' novel, *The Outsider*,[4] where the chief character, Mersault, is ostracized because, out of honesty and sincerity, he could not weep at his mother's funeral.) Here, above all, it is necessary that we share the pain and grief in encouraging the bereaved person to talk about the deceased, to express what he or she truly feels, and to weep.

The second stage shades into the third stage of aimlessness and disorientation, when very often, nothing seems important and worthwhile to the bereaved. But that stage, when the real situation and the necessity for readjustment is beginning to be apparent, is a transitional stage to that (almost comparable to 'rebirth') when the bereaved begins slowly to come through to the final stage of acceptance. Then, she may begin to see that whatever her religious faith, the bereavement is not total loss and that the deceased has become an essential part of her. She will begin to see that she is a different person because of the relationship in which she has been involved and that in itself ensures that there will be no final separation.

These identifiable stages in the process of grieving must not be taken as fitting every experience, nor must we try to put everybody into the framework of the various stages. Too much reliance on the framework may mean that we will miss the particular significance of something that is happening in someone's life. What is helpful is to know that in general, the bereaved go through these stages, with varying depths of intensity, and different time spans. It will mean that we will be able to reassure members of the bereaved's family that the reactions to grief which the bereaved may be suffering are not abnormal – and will eventually pass. Simply to help a person know that what is happening is part of what happens to us all often gives great relief and support. In bereavement, as in other emotional crises, I have found people take immense strength and encouragement from the fact that to the listener what they are experiencing and expressing 'hangs together'. To be reassured of this takes the panic out of the experience and the fear that some mental disturbance is taking place. Of course, the quiet Christian hope of eternal life can be a great sustaining power in bereavement – but it cannot and must not be treated as a substitute for the grieving process through which we all, Christians and others, need to go. Sometimes good Christians have been made to feel guilty if they express grief, as if they were lacking in faith, and that makes the process all the harder to bear.

Lord Hailsham was very illuminating when he was questioned about his feelings on his wife's death:

A lot of people who were believers wrote to one saying, 'Your faith must be a great comfort to you.' Well, I found that it isn't a comfort at all. Faith is not an anaesthetic or an analgesic. You feel just as much pain believing or not believing. The reason one has faith is because of the innate idea, Locke called it, that somewhere the universe makes sense; and your faith is that construct you make round the universe, which is itself a mystery. The Cross wasn't suffered, you know, as a sort of anaesthetic. It was administered without an anaesthetic. That is what unites one to our Lord.[5]

I cannot stress too strongly the necessity for support to be continued right the way through the grief process. As in convalescence, there is a tendency for that support to be withdrawn just at a most critical point: in this case when the pain of the loss is beginning to be most keenly felt. I am thinking of two often-heard sentences: 'She should be getting over it by now,' a sentiment expressed only three or four weeks after the death has occurred, and then, 'She's doing splendidly,' without any questioning about what is going on under the bright exterior, which almost certainly conceals needs that are much better expressed.

There are two groups of people to whom bereavement can be an especially difficult experience. Often, elderly people suffer the loss of their partner just at the time when their contemporaries are leaving them one by one, and their loss is made more stark by a feeling of increasing isolation. Younger people are often faced, not only with many practical problems, and the bringing up of children single-handed, but with the avoidance-techniques others employ and subsequent exclusion from social events since their presence now constitutes an embarrassment. I recall a widow saying to me that being no longer part of a 'socially accepted couple' was one of the hardest things she had to cope with as a widow – and one of the longest lasting.

So, in the process of bereavement, our task as pastoral carers will be directed towards allowing the bereaved time and space and confidence properly to grieve. We will not intrude upon it, or attempt to make them act differently. We are, in the end, developing an atmosphere which helps all concerned to understand what is going on, and respond to it. That means being available, not only to the bereaved herself, but also to the various members of the family who will also be affected by the grieving process. To have someone outside the family with the proper sense of detachment and involvement, who is at hand to absorb the necessary demonstrations of pain and loss, is an incalculable resource.

13

Our Spiritual Resources in Caring

The heart of Christian faith, as I have tried to indicate already, issues directly in our loving and compassionate pastoral care. Our faith in God's unconditional love, which we see supremely in the life, death and risen presence of Jesus, our faith that our love is the strongest force in the world, based on our direct human experience of grace in daily life, will be our chief resource, our final base line when the going gets tough and perseverance is hard.

So what will nourish that love for us and in us? Assuming that we are being fed by those worship-practices which are our custom – whether it be shared sacrament or silence, Bible reading or meditation – then to me it is the 'contemplative spirit' that we most need to cultivate. It is the spirit of looking and seeing, a spirit which issues ultimately both in the vision of God and in more effective ways of caring. Now when I use the phrase 'the vision of God', I am not suddenly taking off into a spiritual fantasy world: it relates to the whole of our Christian journey and the practicalities of our daily life. It goes right back to the beginning of Christian faith and has persisted, with occasional blind spots, ever since. 'Christianity had come into the world with a double purpose, to offer men the Vision of God and to call them to the pursuit of that vision.'[1] So before we had a creed, a doctrine of the Trinity, any fixed liturgical forms, the first post-apostolic theologian was telling us that 'the glory of God is a living man, and the life of man is the Vision of God'.

Jesus specifically related that vision to our everyday experiences. He pictured God at the heart of those experiences in characteristic scenes like children playing in the marketplace, guests at a wedding, farmers sowing in the fields. His unspoken question always seems to have been, 'don't you see?' and this became the spoken question when he wrestled with his friends' lack of understanding: 'You have eyes: can you not see?'[2]

Paul and John take up the theme in the New Testament. Twice Paul uses the metaphor of the mirror[3] to convey the idea of the vision of God increasing our self-knowledge and transforming us into God's likeness. John says that we are simply to look forward to 'see him as he is'.[4] For both, the vision is always related to the person of Christ and whilst its fruition is only in the life to come, we have glimpses of that vision here.

Nicholas of Cusa in the fifteenth century wrote *The Vision of God* to help the monks of a Benedictine abbey focus on the all-seeing God, as if our vision of God is really the business of God seeing us:

> While I look on this pictured face, whether from the east or from the west or the south, it seemeth in like manner itself to look on me, and, after the same fashion, according as I move my face, that face seemeth turned toward me. Even so is thy face turned toward all faces that look upon Thee. Thy glance, Lord, is Thy face. He, then, who looketh on thee with loving face will find thy face looking on himself with love, and the more he shall study to look on thee with greater love, by so much shall he find Thy face more loving.[5]

That vision of God has sometimes been corrupted by excessive personal testimonies of some who claim extravagant mystical experience; and it has often been neglected in the post-Reformation emphasis on hearing the gospel. But the absence of this dimension of seeing leads to a distortion of the gospel. As Simone Weil put it 'One of the principle truths of Christianity, a truth which goes by almost unrecognized today, is that the looking is what saves us.'[6] Ian Ramsey is the modern theologian who has most called our attention to the primacy of vision, this necessity to see. He used to tell how Canon Charles Raven was walking back from Liverpool cathedral on a winter's evening at the time of the early thirties depression in Lancashire, and passed a crowded fish and chip shop. The familiar sight of the shop, the ritual of scooping out the chips and emptying them on to the greaseproof paper and then the newspaper, needs no detailing; but of that customary scene Raven wrote, 'all of a sudden, the glory . . .' The ordinary had become the extraordinary: the proprietor symbolized in that context the Heavenly Father giving his needy children their daily bread. No wonder that Ian Ramsey suggested that 'the place from which all spirituality must begin is the created world around us'.

There are many poets who point to ordinary things and help us to see them and the world 'charged with the grandeur of God'.[7] A particularly good example is the American poet, the late Theodore Roethke, who saw the world as a place enveloped in glory, worthy of the response of reverence for its mystery, a reverence which transfigures even those sights which are distasteful to us. He condemns that rationalizing spirit which is so concerned to intellectualize everything that it misses the dimension of holiness, and fails to see the presence of Being itself, even in a garden slug.

> A mind too active is no mind at all;
> The deep eye sees the shimmer on the stone . . .[8]

Roethke has no wish to moralize on what the deep eye sees: his interest is not in any message that things of creation embody but just that they are. He wants us to see things – and people. He concludes that a poetry which comes from seeing and calls upon the 'lovely diminutives' of the world is a poetry which calls upon God.

Iris Murdoch, both in her philosophical writings and in her novels, illustrates the way in which 'looking', 'seeing', 'attention', is of crucial importance to a rich personal life and is an important way of keeping the self in sober perspective. (In her novels, she often puts *seeing* in italics, in order to emphasize its importance.) She describes an experience of nature she has had which illustrates the point.

> I am looking out of my window in an anxious and resentful state of mind, oblivious of my surroundings, brooding perhaps on some damage done to my prestige. Then suddenly I observe a hovering kestrel. In a moment everything is altered. The brooding self, with its hurt vanity, has disappeared. There is nothing now but kestrel. And when I return to thinking of the other matter it seems less

important. And of course this is something which we may also do deliberately: give attention to nature in order to clear our minds of selfish care.⁹

The same is equally true of art as of nature. Dora in Iris Murdoch's novel, *The Bell*, visits the National Gallery and has a similar experience, contemplating the authority of the pictures 'whose presence destroyed the dreary, trance-like solipsism of her earlier mood'.¹⁰

Now, if you transpose this experience of seeing into a specific religious context, you can see how it fits the contemplative spirit.

Sara Maitland pleads for:

a creative creation theology; one that contemplates, I hope poetically and imaginatively, all the data that our God's creation gives us, looking, not for evidence *for* God, but for the evidence *of* God: the smudges of the divine fingerprint, the stray clues left 'in situ', the brush marks of a great artist, which must inevitably be there, and which – as part of that creation – God has given us the curiosity, the intelligence and the consciousness to explore. Lots of it, to encourage you, is, unsurprisingly but delightfully, very, very beautiful.¹¹

The more our gaze is fixed on God, the more our self-centredness, always poisonous to our caring, shrinks and shrivels. So, silent contemplative exercises can greatly help us. The business of being still and looking at a natural object – it may be a flower, a plant, a winter tree, a picture, a crucifix – for five to ten minutes can help us to cultivate our seeing eye and our openness to different forms, shapes and colours. In this exercise it is quite a common experience to be drawn into and beyond the object of contemplation to that love of God which sustains all things in being.

That looking has direct consequences for our lives and for our caring. Apart from helping us to shed our self concern, when we truly see (a painting, a scene from nature, some object, some person) we afford to the 'other' their proper 'otherness' and autonomy. We cease to judge them or consider their value simply in relation to ourselves. Here, it seems to me, is a wealth of pastoral wisdom: liberation from our self-concern, and self-importance, and an opportunity to see the other person as he or she truly is.

This will also lead us to notice other people, and truly to be noticed is to be allowed space in which to unfold and blossom as a person. Consider: compared with that of other religious reformers the ministry of Jesus appears to have an air of casualness about it. He didn't try to promote any new system of law, or formulate plans for a new and better world order. What he did seems to have been devastatingly simple: he 'makes us see anew the blind man there at the corner, the prostitute in her self-despising, the rich young ruler in his inner emptiness, the old woman in her loneliness. He only shows us the human being next to us.'[12] It was his ability to notice unlikely people that proved for those people the start of a healing process. Of Zachaeus, he was able to say that 'salvation had come to his house'. The woman at the well was left with the words, 'Can this be the Messiah?' on her lips. In the way in which he meets people, he has a powerful healing effect on their whole being so that those who would otherwise feel condemned experience welcome, love, forgiveness – and so healing. When we notice other people, as Jesus met them and took notice of them (and notice, in one sense, is an inadequate word, for it suggests something all too fleeting and trivial) we are offering them hospitality, an open door, a warm welcome, the opportunity to feel at home and be themselves. To be noticed and recognized is to begin again to believe that you have worth – and if human worth, then eternal worth.

The more we see and notice people, the richer will be our intercession, our holding individuals in love in the presence of God. There will be many occasions when seeing someone in need, or hearing of someone who is ill, we will direct an 'arrow prayer' of intercession at God's heart without presuming to tell him what he should do about it. (I've always thought that the authorized version of Mary and Martha's message to Jesus about Lazarus was a perfect example of such an arrow prayer: 'Lord, he whom thou lovest is sick.')[13]

We are much less sceptical than we used to be about the way in which we communicate with one another at the sub-conscious level.

To intercede for another person is to surround that person with a loving atmosphere; it is as if we are providing an oxygen tent in which he is given the space to cope more easily, and feel supported in his life-battles. We may all have different ways of doing this. Some find it helpful to keep intercession lists, in the course of their prayers, with periodic revision, so that each person may be remembered systematically; others, less amenable to such regularity of routine, find it easier to have moments of loving attention at different times in the day. We often say, 'I was only thinking about him, and wondering . . . this morning' and intercessory prayer might well be described as giving our minds to people over a period of time. Most of our ways of looking at prayer have been too unimaginative and inflexible, and the more the complex and hurried life of the twentieth century has impinged on people, the less realistic has become the traditional framework of morning and evening prayers. That is no cause for guilt: it may well be that we are being liberated to enjoy richer experiences.

> What humiliates, looking back at one's attempts at prayer, is the pretentiousness of it all. The elaborate categories which were explained to me when I became a Christian – categories of praise and thanksgiving, of meditation and intercession. One dutifully tried to think oneself into gratitude and penitence and all the rest. I have never quite thrown off the sense of gloom and failure which hung over the whole attempt for me . . . Part of the misery had to do with the talk of relationship with God. I hoped for something not unlike a daily telephone conversation with God and was hurt that he seemed undisposed to chat.[14]

'The daily telephone conversation' which Monica Furlong speaks of here may make prayer sound trivial, but the normality, the taking the reality for granted, the intimacy are all that prayer should surely imply. However else we describe it, prayer is relationship, that which keeps us close to the source of all our caring. Just as in any close human relationship both partners can come to see life and other people through the eyes of the other, so the relationship which is prayer helps us to see and go on seeing other people with and through the eyes of God. And we shall not only begin to see other people as he would see them; we shall begin to see him in them, come to reverence him in them, come to reverence them. No one has expressed this truth, stemming from Jesus' own parable of the sheep and the goats, better than Turgenev, in a most moving piece of literature:

I saw myself, in a dream, a youth, almost a boy, in a low-pitched wooden church. The slim wax candles gleamed, spots of red, before the old pictures of the saints.

A ring of coloured light encircled each tiny flame. Dark and dim it was in the church . . . But there stood before me many people. All fair-haired, peasant heads. From time to time they began swaying, falling, rising again, like the ripe ears of wheat, when the wind of summer passes in slow undulation over them.

All at once some man came up from behind and stood beside me.

I did not turn towards him; but at once I felt that this man was Christ.

Emotion, curiosity, awe overmastered me suddenly. I made an effort . . . and looked at my neighbour.

A face like everyone's face, a face like all men's faces. The eyes looked a little upwards, quietly and intently. The lips closed, but not compressed; the upper lip, as it were, resting on the lower; a small beard parted in two. The hands folded and still. And the clothes on him like everyone's.

'What sort of Christ is this?' I thought. 'Such an ordinary, ordinary man! It can't be!'

I turned away. But I had hardly turned my eyes away from this ordinary man when I felt again that it really was none other than Christ standing beside me.

Again I made an effort over myself . . . And again the same face, like all men's faces, the same everyday though unknown features.

And suddenly my heart sank, and I came to myself. Only then

I realized that just such a face – a face like all men's faces – is the face of Christ.[15]

Such a reverence for the person, such a transfiguration of the ordinary: that is the heart of true pastoral care.

14

Ourselves as Carers

One Saturday evening, forty years ago, I had a moment of great illumination in a small Carlisle theatre. The resident repertory company was performing Graham Greene's first play, *The Living Room*. There was a passage towards the end of the play in which Rose Pemberton, desperate in her fight for her love of a married man against the conventions of the church and society in which she had been reared, is in conversation with her uncle James, a Catholic priest.

> I just want a bit of ordinary human comfort. Not formulas. 'Love God.' 'Trust God.' 'Everything will be alright one day.' Uncle, *please* say something that's not Catholic.[1]

(And Catholic, of course, means nothing more than doctrinally orthodox or sound. Had Rose been of another persuasion, the word *Protestant* would have been equally valid.) And when Rose is finally driven to the brink of suicide because of the state of moral confusion in which she finds herself, her uncle – trying hard to leap over the gulf which separates his cool orthodoxies from her passionate experience of life – confesses that all he has to offer is 'the Penny Catechism'. 'There's always the mass,' he says, 'There's your Rosary . . . perhaps our Lady'. And then, in one final fling of despair – 'Prayer'.[2] But uncle James does not need convincing of the barrenness of his own case and the sleeping tablets lie too close to Rose's hands.

To my shame, I realized then for the first time the folly of a patronizing response to deep personal needs with the repetition of religious formulae, which have degenerated into being hardly more than clichés, and which do not begin to touch the reality or depth of those needs. I determined from then on that I would try only to use religious statements which made sense in people's lives, illuminate some of their darkness and aid them in their personal struggles.

That evening taught me something else. It opened my eyes to the enriching of pastoral care through the medium of modern drama and modern novels. I say 'modern drama' and 'modern novels', not because the classics are not equally profitable; but because the people for whom we care are set in the same late-twentieth-century context as the characters of whom we read and face the same pressures of the age. When talking on the subject to adult Christian groups, I have often been dismayed by their nervous reaction, as if I were suggesting something very risky both to faith and morals. My experience is that, however 'earthy' some of these plays and novels are in tone and language, they can open the eyes even of those who have taken little interest in literature, as they portray in flesh and blood form those questions which lie just under the surface of their lives. It isn't necessarily that they confirm their faith; indeed, it may be that some will be led to a process of questioning that faith, which can only in the long run be healthy. But if we are going to feel on our pulse what is going on underneath the surface of peoples' lives, and so enable ourselves to show a greater empathy with them, then such involvement is essential. Of course, many of us may not have many opportunities for theatregoing, but reading and pondering such plays can be a good second best and in any case, if we are able to be theatregoers, reading the play afterwards is a bonus and doubles the value of it all. My hope would be that if we use some of our leisure time this way, we shall find not only enjoyment in the plays but stimulation to more fruitful pastoral care.

I have hinted earlier than a sad feature of the contemporary church in its fight for survival, and its institutional concerns, is its neglect of the road to holiness, our personal growth in sheer goodness. So it comes as something of a judgment on us to find that the contemporary theatre has often explored, and sometimes expressed, this concept of the 'good person'. David Hare's play *Racing Demon* portrays the overworked and under-rewarded inner-city parish priest, Lionel, who still goes on determinedly believing that 'a priest should be like any other man. Only full of love'.[3] And the central character of Hare's play *The Secret Rapture* depicts Isobel giving herself away for the sake of others. She talks of having 'made a commitment' to Katherine and asks 'Why should I drop it because the going gets hard? The great thing is to love, if you're loved back it's a bonus.'[4] Alan Ayckbourn, known more for comedy than social comment, paints a picture of a seemingly (but only seemingly) naive man, in *Man of the Moment*, Douglas. When asked by a cynical TV presenter what he feels strongly about, Douglas simply says, 'I suppose evil, really.'[5] Even the much misunderstood Harold Pinter, whose plays are usually associated in the popular mind with banality and obscurity, is capable of giving voice to 'unspoken fears, sufferings and yearnings shared by all mankind'.[6]

Two more recent plays are full of spiritual and pastoral resonances. Arthur Miller's play *Broken Glass*[7] takes its title from Kristallnacht in November 1938, the night when the Nazis went on the rampage and broke Jewish shop windows and looted their contents. Sylvia, the wife of a successful Jew, is stricken with a paralysis of the legs for no discernible medical reason, but is obviously obsessed by the stories coming out of Germany, especially about those elderly Jews who are being forced to scrub the pavements with toothbrushes. The correlation between the physical paralysis and the situation in Germany symbolizes the spiritual paralysis most of us feel when confronted with the spectacle of appalling suffering and evil. This continues to be a difficulty today for so many good and caring people who cannot square their uneasy consciences simply by giving a donation for some charitable cause or including in their intercessions those who are suffering most. But faith doesn't require of us the impossible, especially since there are so many good causes in which to be involved – and it also tells us that it doesn't all depend on us! Much as we might wish it, we cannot take on the burdens of the whole world, and realistically, perhaps, we do more good by concentrating on one or two areas or groups of people who need strong support than by exhausting ourselves in spreading ourselves too thinly over the whole world. (Public intercession in church sometimes becomes wearisome for the same reason. A colleague of mine once remarked that he felt a suitable introduction to some intercessions might be 'God, as you read in the *Financial Times* last Monday . . .')

Another play which resonates pastorally, especially at a time of an increasingly elderly population, is that by Edward Albee, *Three Tall Women*,[8] for witty and comic as it often is, it faces the two subjects of senescence and death, subjects which are usually evaded, sanitized, or sentimentalized. In the words of the ninety-year-old A (the character is called just A), 'There's a difference between knowing you're going to *die* and *knowing* you're going to die. The second is better; it moves away from the theoretical.' And as we have already seen when we were exploring terminal care, the second is not only better, it's crucial if we are going to be able to care properly and not be caught up in our own conflicts with the dying process.

Similarly, modern novels can stretch our imagination and nourish our empathy. I had an experience similar to my theatre experience in Carlisle when I sat on a park bench in the sunshine in Toronto on a summer's day in 1963 and read at one sitting the novel by Albert Camus, *The Outsider*.[9] It was shock to the system to become aware of the way in which our lives are so much ruled by convention and by so-called 'tact', and to read of the author's comment that in the leading character, Mersault, he portrays 'the only Christ we deserve'. But all the novels of Camus are equally stimulating and richly rewarding. His novel, *The Fall*,[10] was a searing illustration of the insidious nature of guilt and its effect on human beings, and makes the point that not even Christ was immune from the guilt of the human condition since, indirectly, he was responsible for the massacre of the innocents at his birth. Other writers spring equally to mind. Iris Murdoch, for instance, explores in her character Stuart Cuno in *The Good Apprentice* the possibility of becoming good without God. He has this 'instinctive craving for nothingness which was also a desire to be able to love and enjoy and "touch" everything; to *help* everything'.[11] William Golding's contention that 'man produces evil as a bee produces honey' is well seen in the sin of overweening pride and ambition in his novel *The Spire*.[12]

Or take this example from Ian McEwan's novel, *A Child in Time*. There is a painful immediacy about his writing, described by one critic as 'a godly sense of awareness', which like all good writing has the power to engender the sensory experience it describes. In one striking passage, McEwan reflects on this awareness. Stephen Lewis is visiting a friend and walking through the wood which borders his garden. It is a jungle of moss and lichen, a sort of miniature Amazon. For the moment he felt quite overwhelmed. Kate, his daughter, has been abducted in a supermarket and he muses about what her reaction to the garden might be.

It needed a child, Stephen thought, succumbing to the inevitable. Kate would not be aware of the car half a mile behind, or of the wood's perimeters and all that lay beyond them, roads, opinions, Government. The wood, this spider rotating on its thread, this beetle lumbering over blades of grass would be all, the moment would be everything. He needed her good influence, her lessons in celebrating the specific: how to fill the present and be filled by it to the point where identity faded to nothing. He was always partly somewhere else, never quite paying attention, never wholly serious. Wasn't that Nietzsche's idea of true maturity, to attain the seriousness of a child at play?[13]

I could go on quoting more examples but that would be self indulgent. I hope that by now you are convinced that modern literature offers you in your leisure, not only much enjoyment but indirectly, the enlarging of your awareness and self-awareness, qualities essential in our caring. But I cannot resist quoting just one more example, not necessarily because it stretches our imagination and nourishes our empathy, but simply because its humorous approach to counselling helps us to laugh at ourselves and maintain a sense of proportion about ourselves. It is David Hare's recent play *Skylight*. Tom's wife has died a year ago and he is explaining to his friend how he was offered support in his bereavement.

A woman came – I didn't tell you this – a woman came to the door.

She said she was from a local support group. I couldn't believe it. She told me she'd come to help me to grieve. I said, 'I beg your pardon?' She said, don't worry, it's not going to cost you. It's on the rates. Or the Poll Tax, whatever it's called. I said 'I'm meant to feel better? You mean that's meant to make it all right? That's meant to make all the difference? Oh, good, this is great, I think I'll do this, I'll mourn my wife in the company of this total stranger. After all it's going to be *free* . . .' I said, 'Look, lady, I'll tell you one thing. When I choose to grieve for this woman . . . this woman with whom I spent such a . . . such a *large* part of my life, it will not be in the presence of a member of Wimbledon Council.' She said, 'Oh we're in Merton now.'[14]

Tom then has a moment of great insight:

I mean, please tell me, what is it? Don't they know anything? You suffer. That's what you do. There are no short cuts. There are no easy ways. And I have been doing my share of suffering.[15]

Such an ability to laugh at ourselves is essential. I am really suggesting that the more relaxed we are about our own motivation, the better carers we shall be. In my more mischievous moments, in the midst of many earnest discussions about being 'useful', I sometimes feel like protesting our uselessness, since it is 'the uselessness of being' which may accomplish more than much 'useful doing', and bring a little warm humanity to what we are.

I like the old Chinese story I once heard about the carpenter and the apprentice. They were walking together through a huge forest, when they came across a very tall, beautiful, old and gnarled tree. The carpenter asked the apprentice whether he knew why the tree was so tall and beautiful. And when the apprentice said that he didn't, the carpenter replied, 'Because it is useless. If it had been useful it would have been cut down ages ago and made into tables and chairs, but because it's useless it could grow so tall and so beautiful that people can sit in its shade and relax.'

We as carers should, above all, be those who can enable others to sit in our shade and relax. Carl Gustav Jung, surely a professional among professionals, used to say that if he wanted to treat a patient psychologically, he had to give up all pretensions to authority or superior knowledge, or any wish to influence. The deadly enemy of caring is earnestness, that humourless determination which wants you to hand over the running of your life on the grounds that they know best. And even if they did it would be an inadequate reason for making such a handover. It is very sad when well-intentioned, blameless characters are frustrated in their good works because their very earnestness proves an obstacle to other people and far from encouraging them to seek help, makes them withdraw still further. ('Hide me from those who want to help.') I well remember how someone described the character of two earnest missionaries at work in East Africa. 'They tried so hard, they became unlovely in their trying . . .'

Now it might sound as if I am advocating a degree of indifference or lack of commitment. Not a bit of it. Earnestness, gritting ones' teeth in self-endeavour, is ultimately a sign of a certain absence of faith rather than its presence. It is to be persuaded that if I don't do it, no one else will and that consequently not only the other person, but God himself, cannot manage without me. Other people are not in our hands but in his. Of course, some emergencies will arise in which we shall need to act with intense concentration and resolution, but even then we need not be frightened or perturbed. 'To care and not to care' properly is a lesson to be learned and it is a lesson in faith.

What then do we need? What resources will enable us to keep our sensitivity in our caring? We all need to be able to open ourselves up to another person in whom we have complete trust, who can help us assess our motives, for instance, and who knows us well enough to see what is really going on inside us. Some of us may be fortunate enough to have a friend, whether a member of the church or not, who will be ready and willing to do this for us. But assume for a moment that that is not the case. What are the implications for the church as a local community of carers? Ought it not to provide just that sort of resource, that level of personal involvement with each other? Recently, a question that has received some attention in the helping professions is: who helps the helpers? Is the high suicide rate among psychiatrists at least partly attributable to the way in which involvement in other peoples' dilemmas at a deep sub-conscious level shows up the chaos in their own personal lives, a chaos which isn't, for professional reasons and reasons of confidentiality, able to be shared with other people? Where do social workers with heavy caseloads find release and sources of refreshment and renewal? Does there exist a structure of pastoral care in our churches (especially in those which pride themselves on having bishops as pastors), which enables clergymen and ministers to be freed from the isolation their position often seems to impose, and gives them a real chance to speak of their own fears, frustrations and loneliness? From my own limited experience, the answer to the last question is, sadly, negative. But what is a body of carers about if it doesn't mutually share in the caring, if people don't care for one another? And if my assumption that the church is such a community of carers is right, then what does this presuppose for the organization of church life? What is important is to be given the opportunity to share in our caring concern, and all that has been too tragically missing from the life of the church in general for too long. If caring were just about 'practical matters', for bustling, zealous, breathless disciples, then it wouldn't matter: but since caring is as much a matter of the mind and emotions as it is of the will to serve, then it matters a great deal that an outlet for quiet thought, sharing in concern together, reflection on action, is always available. And lest that, again, creates an impression of over-seriousness and furrowed brows, it should be stressed that the value of such a group will be to take some of the heat out of the common problems, to help people to laugh together and relax.

That brings us to a characteristic danger of all pastoral caring. Inevitably, most of our caring is to do with the negative side of life, offering support in and through times of personal crisis and we may begin to assume that Christian concern is only with such areas of life. Dietrich Bonhoeffer, looking out from his prison cell at the way Christian faith shows itself in the world, realized the danger:

God must be recognized at the centre of life, not when we are at the end of our resources; it is his will to be recognized in life, and not only when death comes; in health and vigour, and not only in suffering; in our activities, and not only in sin.[16]

The inherent difficulty for full-time professional carers is that their time is so taken up with the ambulance side of life that it is sometimes very difficult to keep a balance. Life becomes distorted, and the temptation is simply to seek release through the artificial escapism afforded by drink and drugs. In our pastoral care, we are much more bound up with different life experiences and our other involvements may prevent such distortion. Even so, any concentration on the negative side of life tends to make us believe that God is to be found only through suffering. This so colours our attitude that we are less effective than we might be, for those who are beset by problems inevitably see their problems and the resolution of them as being the key to the whole of life, and our intentness can squeeze out the possibility of beauty, trust, spontaneity, and fun. It is just that dimension with which they need to be in touch, and it is our wholeness as carers which will ensure it. The attitude of 'I'm a carer; you can see if you look at my furrowed brow and worried expression' needs to be dispelled. Of course, the opposite of that, the perpetual grinning expression which continually invites you to cheer up, is equally unhelpful.

The characteristic Christian quality of joy is neither. Sarah Maitland, in describing the origin of the word 'joy' as 'jewel', says of it that it is 'the treasure buried in the field, the pearl of great price'.[17] Joy is independent of time and circumstance, does not necessarily arise as a successful outcome of a particular event, but is nourished by an underlying faith in God's love, whatever the circumstances, and can from time to time bubble over spontaneously. In the New Testament, joy often occurs in the context of suffering and separation. It was for the joy that was set before him, we're told, that Jesus endured the cross and it was when he was speaking of his own going away that he also said, 'no one shall rob you of your joy'.[18] Abraham Maslow discovered through his research that one important factor contributing to the maturity of people was frequent experience of this spontaneous 'bubbling over'. But we can develop neither the steady flame nor the 'peak experiences of joy' merely by willing them, or wishing them. The flame grows as we nurture our faith in God's love; the 'peak experience' comes uninvited, and the most we can do is to be sensitive to it, to be ready to realize it and let it do its work for us. Like happiness, joy is a by-product which flows from a sense of the worthwhileness and the wholeness of life and it is always a surprise.

We will be open, then, to the experience of joy, not only on our own account, but also because joy is an important quality which the 'cared for' will sense in the carer for the sake of his or her own recovery and health. To speak directly of joy to someone in the grip of misery or despair would be cruel; to be able to communicate joy indirectly is to open the door of hope for another person, the hope that out of the present concentration on stress, a new wholeness will emerge.

Joy, then, cannot be sought directly; but there is an important way of preparing for it, and it is to do with giving ourselves time to appreciate unhurriedly experiences open to us. The more we give of our time, energy and concentration to other people, the more time we need by ourselves – and this may well be misunderstood as selfishness. What I am sure we do need is to have a leisure interest and hobby which is nothing to do with caring. (Having said that, I will add that my hobby is bird watching and indirectly, of course, it must help me to *see* better!) The richer, fuller and more mature a person I am the more I have to give as I stretch out my hand to others. The more I have to give – of myself.

Finally, a word of great encouragement. We are living, and will increasingly live, in a world of dehumanizing tendencies, a world where very often people escape involvement with each other, and treat that delicate and mysterious organism which is the human person with indifference, if not contempt. Every time we stretch out our hand in caring, we make an act of faith in the widest sense of that word. Our caring and counselling may never be impressive statistically and of the most fruitful of our encounters we will probably never know the outcome. But in this dehumanizing society we are, in our caring, asserting the unique value of the person in all his or her many-sidedness, and especially in the matter of relationships. We are maintaining that the way individuals act, care, and are, will always be significant, and more still, we are making a vital contribution to the healing of the whole world.

Parable . . .

(for self-examination by every local church . . .)

On a dangerous seacoast where shipwrecks often occur there was once a crude little lifesaving station. The building was just a hut, and there was only one boat, but the few devoted members kept a constant watch over the sea, and with no thought for themselves went out day and night tirelessly searching for the lost. Many lives were saved by this wonderful little station, so that it became famous. Some of those who were saved, and various others in the surrounding area, wanted to become associated with the station and give of their time and money and effort for the support of its work. New boats were bought and new crews trained. The little lifesaving station grew.

Some of the members of the lifesaving station were unhappy that the building was so crude and poorly equipped. They felt that a more comfortable place should be provided as the first refuge of those saved from the sea. So they replaced the emergency cots with beds and put better furniture in the enlarged building. Now the lifesaving station became a popular gathering place for its members, and they decorated it beautifully and furnished it exquisitely, because they used it as a sort of club. Fewer members were now interested in going to sea on lifesaving missions, so they hired lifeboat crews to do this work. The lifesaving motif still prevailed in the club's decoration, and there was a liturgical lifeboat in the room where the club initiations were held. About this time a large ship was wrecked off the coast, and the hired crews brought in boatloads of cold, wet and half-drowned people. They were dirty and sick, and some of them had black skin and some had yellow skin. The beautiful new club was in chaos. So the property committee immediately had a shower house built outside the club where victims of shipwreck could be cleaned up before coming inside.

At the next meeting, there was a split in the club membership. Most of the members wanted to stop the club's lifesaving activities as being unpleasant and a hindrance to the normal social life of the club. Some members insisted upon lifesaving as their primary purpose and pointed out that they were still called a lifesaving station. But they were finally voted down and told that if they wanted to save the lives of all the various kinds of people who were shipwrecked in those waters, they could begin their own lifesaving station down the coast. They did.

As the years went by, the new station experienced the same changes that had occurred in the old. It evolved into a club, and yet another lifesaving station was founded. History continued to repeat itself, and if you visit that sea coast today, you will find a number of exclusive clubs along that shore. Shipwrecks are frequent in those waters, but most of the people drown![1]

Another Parable . . .

(for encouragement . . .)

A few years ago, a Scottish lady, we'll call her Mrs Campbell, went in search of her husband who'd left her because, as he said, he kept letting her down through drink. All she knew, through a postcard he'd sent her, was that he was somewhere in the Manchester area. It was a cold wet afternoon in early January when, after a rail journey from Glasgow, she stepped off what was then a number 48 bus, into a murky, traffic-crowded Manchester street. She'd never been out of Scotland before, she had a pound in her pocket, she had no bed for the night and no friend to whom she could turn. The bus-stop was just outside the church, a large, galleried Victorian edifice which, if you could look at it objectively, you'd say was rather ugly. But it was open, it was warm and the light of the Christmas crib was sufficient for our Scottish lady to see her way inside. Mrs Campbell sat down in the quiet of the church and pondered, leaving her considerable baggage under the pew. Presently Mrs Andrews, a member of the congregation and Mothers' Union, came in – not alas, to pray, though of course she wouldn't have dreamt of going away without – but in order to put a copy of *Readers' Digest* on the table – her monthly present for the rector, since she had been given two Christmas gift subscriptions. It was a strange subdued conversation which ensued when Mrs Andrews caught sight of Mrs Campbell – and poor Mrs Andrews never realized what she was in for when the innocent thought of the rector's *Readers' Digest* entered her head. For she found herself taking Mrs Campbell to her already overcrowded home for the night with her essential requisites, whilst she left her baggage under the pew, muttering, 'It'll be all right there.' They managed. But the next day, to ease the accommodation problem, Mrs Andrews asked a disabled lady from the church and her sister, living just across the road from the building, to see what they could do. It was sufficient simply to be asked; no more conditions were necessary. They gave Mrs Campbell the room they had, with an enormous double bed and 'Home Sweet Home' in Gothic lettering above the bed for good measure. The three of them got on so well that Mrs Campbell felt able to confide in them, and tell her little story, which was received with great sympathy and many unhelpful suggestions. Soon Mrs Campbell became attracted to the daily offices of the church; she would persist in standing when others were sitting and sitting when others were kneeling. No matter . . . and she soon had several people in the church doing detective work in and around the area, searching for her vagrant husband. It was ten days later when one or two members of the parish saw her, two days after she had given herself another three days in which to find her man. There she was, triumphantly striding along the busy street, her man (considerably smaller than she was) trotting at her side, obediently carrying the large suitcase.

That true story, from an ordinary Manchester parish, is such a glorious parable of what the church is. Mrs Campbell found the church open and warm, and she wouldn't have looked at it twice if it hadn't been. She came across ordinary people in an everyday situation spontaneously caring, in what (to the world at least) would be an extraordinary way. She was accepted, as herself – and with no strings attached, she was helped. No questions about her past life; no catechizing about her religious affiliations. And the result? Nothing will shake her now in her conviction that the church really is the Body of Christ, stretching out his arms to draw, to heal, to bring together, the place where we really *belong*. Obviously, Mrs Campbell's story doesn't represent the *end* of all our pastoral caring in the church; but it might be a beginning . . .

Notes and Suggestions for Further Reading

1. Fixed and Changing Contexts of Pastoral Care

1. Stephen Sykes, *Unashamed Anglicanism*, Darton, Longman & Todd 1995, p. 221.
2. I John 4.19.
3. Romans 5.8.
4. Alastair Campbell, *Paid to Care*, SPCK 1985, p. 1.
5. Mark 8.35.
6. Mark 8.35.
7. Stephen Pattison, *Pastoral Care and Liberation Theology*, CUP 1994.

2. Human Needs and our Response

1. A. H. Maslow, *Motivation and Personality*, Harper Bros, New York 1970.
2. II Thessalonians 3.10.

3. Caring and Growth

1. V. A. Demant, *The Responsibility and Scope of Pastoral Theology Today*, OUP 1950, p. 5.
2. R. A. Lambourne in *Contact*, no. 35 (1971).
3. I Corinthians 13.11.
4. Ephesians 4.14.
5. Romans 8.29.
6. H. A. Williams, *True Wilderness*, Constable 1965, pp. 158–9.
7. Matthew 5.48.
8. Diana Collins, *Partners in Protest*, Cassell 1992.
9. Marina Chavhavadze (ed), *Man's Concern for Holiness*, Hodder and Stoughton 1970, p. 26.
10. Paul C. Vitz, *Psychology and Religion: The Cult of Self-Worship*, Eerdmans, Grand Rapids 1977, pp. 91, 95.

11. Matthew 6.7.

4. *Ambiguities in our Caring*

1. Monica Furlong, *God's a Good Man and Other Poems*, Mowbray 1974, p. 62.
2. Sidney Jourard, *The Transparent Self*, D. Van Nostrand, New York 1971, p. 182.
3. Brian Clark, *Whose Life is it Anyway?*, Amber Lane Press 1978, pp. 29–31.
4. Ibid., p. 34.
5. Ibid., p. 54.
6. *Christian Believing*. A Report by the Doctrine Commission of the Church of England, SPCK 1976, p. 3.

5. *Counselling Insights in Pastoral Care*

1. *Counselling*, Journal of the British Association for Counselling, vol. 6, no. 1, 1995, p. 39.
2. II Corinthians 5.21.
3. Dietrich Bonhoeffer, *Life Together*, SCM Press 1954, p. 75.
4. Brian Thorne, *Person-Centred Counselling*, Whurr Publishers, London & New York 1991, p. 81.
5. Ibid., p. 76.
6. H. A. Williams, *True Resurrection*, Mitchell Beazley 1972, p. 115.

6. *Pastoral Care at Work*

1. *The Times*, 11 June 1988.
2. Dietrich Bonhoeffer, *Prisoner for God*, Macmillan 1957, p. 140.
3. I John 4.19.
4. Matthew 7.21.
5. Colin Morris, *God-in-a-Box*, Hodder & Stoughton 1984, p. 229.

7. *Our Relationships*

1. Edward Albee, *The Zoo Story*, Penguin Books 1965, pp. 174f.
2. Iris Murdoch, 'The Idea of Perfection' *in The Sovereignty of Good*, Routledge & Kegan Paul 1970, pp. 43f.
3. Tony Lake, *Relationships*, Michael Joseph 1981, pp. 27–32.
4. George Herbert, 'Constancy' in e.g. *Works of George Herbert*, F. E. Hutchinson (ed), Clarendon Press 1941, pp. 72f.
5. *The Guardian*, 12 June 1995.

6. Matthew 12. 48–50.
7. See *Something to Celebrate*, Church House Publishing 1995.
8. Robert Bolt, *A Man for All Seasons*, Heinemann 1960, Act II.

8. Our Three Ages

1. Rollo May, *The Courage to Create*, Bantam Books, New York 1975, pp. 138f.
2. Ronald Blythe, *The View in Winter*, Penguin Books 1981.

9. Our Grey Areas

1. Gerald Priestland, *My Pilgrim Way*, Mowbray 1993, p. 114 and 116–7.
2. Gordon Allport, *The Person in Psychology*, Beacon Press, Boston 1968, pp. 131f.

10. Pastoral Care in Illness

1. Luke 11.19.
2. John 5.6.
3. Geoffrey Lampe, *Explorations in Theology 8*, SCM Press 1981, p. 21.
4. Romans 8.19 (AV).
5. Leonard Hodgson, *For Faith and Freedom* Vol. II, Basil Blackwell 1957, reissued in one vol. SCM Press 1968, p. 131.
6. Mark 10.52.
7. Paul Tillich, *The New Being*, SCM Press 1963, pp. 38–9.
8. John 9.3.
9. II Corinthians 12.7.
10. J. K. Smith, *Free Fall*, SPCK 1977.
11. Charles Causley, 'Ten Types of Hospital Visitor', *Collected Poems 1951–1975*, Macmillan 1975, p. 248.
12. Vincent Brummer, *What Are We Doing When We Pray?*, SCM Press 1984, p. 57.
13. Monica Furlong, *Contemplating Now*, Hodder & Stoughton 1971, pp. 67–8.

11. Pastoral Care of the Terminally Ill

1. Lily Pincus, *The Challenge of a Long Life*, Faber & Faber 1981, p. 123.
2. Glin Bennett, *Patients and their Doctors*, Ballière Tindall 1979, p. 129.
3. Dennis Potter, *Seeing the Blossom*, Faber & Faber 1994, p. 5.
4. Sheila Cassidy, *Light from the Dark Valley*, Darton, Longman & Todd 1994, p. 131.

12. *Pastoral Care of the Bereaved*

1. Dietrich Bonhoeffer, *Ethics*, SCM Press 1955; revised edition 1971, pp. 103–4.
2. Susan Hill, *In the Springtime of the Year*, Hamish Hamilton 1974.
3. Luke 23.34.
4. Albert Camus, *The Outsider*, Penguin Books 1961.
5. Lord Hailsham in Bel Mooney, *Perspectives for Living: Conversations on Bereavement and Love*, John Murray 1992, p. 72.

13. *Our Spiritual Resources in Caring*

1. Kenneth Kirk, *The Vision of God*, James Clark 1977, p. 1.
2. Mark 8.17.
3. I Corinthians 13.13 and II Corinthians 3.10.
4. I John 3.2.
5. Nicholas of Cusa, *The Vision of God*, from Atlantic Paperbacks edition, p. 24.
6. Simone Weil, *Waiting on God*, Routledge & Kegan Paul 1951, p. 125.
7. See Gerald Manley Hopkins' poem 'God's Grandeur'.
8. Theodore Roethke, *The Collected Poems of Theodore Roethke*, Faber & Faber 1968, p. 244.
9. Iris Murdoch, *The Sovereignty of Good*, Routledge & Kegan Paul 1970, p. 84.
10. Iris Murdoch, *The Bell*, Chatto & Windus 1958, p. 192.
11. Sara Maitland, *A Big-Enough God*, Mowbray 1995, p. 15.
12. Helmut Theilicke, *How the World Began*, James Clarke 1964, p. 200.
13. John 11.3.
14. Monica Furlong, *Travelling In*, Hodder & Stoughton 1971, p. 52.
15. Quoted in Victor Gollancz, *A Year of Grace*, Gollancz 1950, pp. 51f. from Ivan Turgenev, *Dream Tales and Prose Poems* ed. Constance Garrett, Heinemann.

14. *Ourselves as Carers*

1. Graham Greene, *The Living Room*, Heinemann 1953, p. 49.
2. Ibid., p. 58.
3. David Hare, *Racing Demon*, Faber & Faber 1990, p. 68.
4. David Hare, *The Secret Rapture*, Faber & Faber 1988, p. 78.
5. Alan Ayckbourn, *Man of the Moment*, Faber & Faber 1980, p. 19.
6. Martin Esslin, *The People's Wound*, Methuen 1970, p. 235.
7. Arthur Miller, *Broken Glass*, Methuen 1994.
8. Edward Albee, *Three Tall Women*, Penguin 1995, p. 109.

9. Albert Camus, *The Outsider*, Penguin 1963.
10. Albert Camus, *The Fall*, Penguin 1963.
11. Iris Murdoch, *The Good Apprentice*, Penguin, p. 55.
12. William Golding, *The Spire*, Faber & Faber 1964.
13. Ian McEwan, *The Child in Time*, Jonathan Cape 1987, pp. 105–6.
14. David Hare, *Skylight*, Faber & Faber 1995, pp. 47–8.
15. Ibid., p. 48.
16. Dietrich Bonhoeffer, *Letters and Papers from Prison*, The Enlarged Edition, SCM Press 1971, p. 312.
17. Sara Maitland, *A Big-Enough God*, Mowbray 1995, p. 166.
18. John 16.22.

Parable

1. Based on a parable by Theodore O. Wedel and quoted by H. J. Clinebell Jr in *Basic Types of Pastoral Care and Counselling*, Abingdon Press, Nashville and SCM Press, London 1984, pp. 13f.

Here are some books for further exploration:

Bridger, Francis and Atkinson, David, *Counselling in Context*, HarperCollins 1994.
Campbell, Alastair V., *Paid to Care*, SPCK 1985.
Forrester, Duncan B., *Theology and Practice*, Epworth Press 1990.
Jacobs, Michael, *Faith or Fear?*, Darton, Longman & Todd 1987.
Leech, Kenneth, *Soul Friend*, Darton, Longman & Todd 1994.
Mayne, Michael, *The Sunrise of Wonder*, HarperCollins 1995.
Thorne, Brian, *Person-Centred Counselling*, Whurr 1991.
Wilson, Michael, *A Coat of Many Colours*, Epworth Press 1988.